MATH
By All Means®

PLACE VALUE
Grades 1–2

MATH
By All Means ®

PLACE VALUE
Grades 1–2

by Marilyn Burns
A MARILYN BURNS REPLACEMENT UNIT

MATH SOLUTIONS PUBLICATIONS

Editorial Direction: Lorri Ungaretti
Design: Aileen Friedman
Page makeup: Aileen Friedman and David Healy, First Image
Cover background and border design: Barbara Gelfand

Marilyn Burns Education Associates is dedicated to improving mathematics education. For information about Math Solutions courses, resource materials, and other services, write or call:

Marilyn Burns Education Associates
150 Gate 5 Road, Suite 101
Sausalito, CA 94965
Telephone (415) 332-4181
Fax (415) 331-1931

This unit was developed by Marilyn Burns and Bonnie Tank as part of a year-long second-grade mathematics curriculum development project conducted by Marilyn Burns Education Associates.

ISBN 0-941355-09-8

This book is printed on recycled paper.

Distributed by Cuisenaire Company of America, Inc.
P.O. Box 5026
White Plains, NY 10602-5026
(800) 237-3142

PREFACE

For the two school years before writing this book, I taught math to a class of second graders. I was in the classroom for an hour each day, from 11:05 to 12:05, after second recess and before lunch. Although I wasn't the children's "regular teacher," I was the their "regular math teacher," and I assumed full responsibility for planning and teaching.

I organized the year's instruction into units and spent five to six weeks on each. The units did not enrich or supplement what appeared in current second-grade textbooks but, instead, replaced textbook instruction and embraced an alternative approach to math teaching. This place-value unit represents the work I did with the class from the third week of October until Thanksgiving vacation. It's a completely developed plan for teaching second grade children about place value.

While the book presents a replacement unit for only a five-week period in second grade, my purpose for writing it is much broader. The unit is a model that can be applied to math instruction at all grades to address how the goals and guidelines of the current reform movement in school mathematics can translate to classroom instruction. As with each *Math By All Means* book, the application of this replacement unit is specific, but its pedagogical intent reaches much further.

The unit has three central elements. One is a broadened interpretation of mathematics instruction. The primary focus of the unit is on helping children make sense of our place value system of numbers. However, the activities draw from other areas of the mathematics curriculum, including statistics, geometry, and measurement.

A second element central to the unit is the notion that students are the constructors and interpreters of their own understanding. To this end, the lessons engage students in exploring ideas, solving problems, making conjectures, investigating patterns, inventing procedures, and communicating

about their thinking and reasoning, both orally and in writing. The goal of the unit is to have children construct for themselves understanding of place value.

A third key aspect is the importance of the role of the teacher. The unit provides complete teaching instructions, but students in other classes will react differently from the reactions I've reported. Also, teachers' styles differ. Therefore, I believe that teachers must make professional choices when teaching, and I encourage you to adapt, mold, and personalize the unit.

Although I taught for only an hour each day, I found the experience totally consuming. I kept daily logs. When a day went well, I left singing and cheerfully typed detailed notes about all that happened. When a day was difficult, I left feeling discouraged, perplexed, sometimes miserable. I labored over my log, wondering if the effort of teaching was worth it.

I can now say, without hesitation, that the experience was worth the effort. I've spent many hours poring over the children's work, taking the time that wasn't available to me while I was immersed in preparations for daily instruction. I'm astounded at how much I've learned—both about students' learning and my teaching—from studying those papers.

Along with providing the information needed to teach the unit, I've tried to include my insights and reactions. I hope that this unit helps you see how to provide place value instruction that engages second graders, helps them construct understanding of our number system, and encourages them to develop an appreciation for mathematics. I welcome your feedback.

All of the "From the Classroom" vignettes describe what happened when the unit was taught in a second-grade class. However, the grade level span assigned to the unit indicates that it is suitable for grades one and two. We've made this grade-level designation for two reasons. We know that in any class, there is typically a span in students' interests and abilities, and the activities in the unit have been designed to respond to such a span. Also, teachers who have taught the unit have found it successful with children in several grade levels and have reported that the activities are accessible and appropriate to a range of students.

Marilyn Burns
January 1994

Acknowledgments

Special thanks to the teachers and children in whose classes the unit was tested.

Park School, Mill Valley School District, California

Chapter 1 Mathematics Project Schools, Tucson Unified School District, Arizona

Wildwood School, San Francisco Unified School District, California

Alamo School, San Francisco Unified School District, California

CONTENTS

Introduction   1

Assessments   13

    Individual Interviews   17
    Numbers on the 0–99 Chart   36
    How Many 10s?   67
    How Much is Covered?   116
    Catherine's Problem   140

Whole Class Lessons   21

    The 0–99 Chart   22
    Stars in One Minute   41
    Counting Fish   56
    The King's Commissioners   72

Menu Activities   83

    Race for $1.00   92
    Dollar Signs   101
    Cover a Flat   110
    0–99 Patterns   122
    Number Puzzle   129
    Fill the Cube   134
    Make a Shape   146
    Five Tower Game   152
    Guess My Number   160

Children's Books   167

Draw Me a Star   168
The Go-Around Dollar   168
The King's Commissioners   169

Homework   171

Stars in One Minute   172
Dollar Signs   172
Race for $1.00   173
Number Puzzle   174
Guess My Number   175

Blackline Masters   177

Place Value Menu   178
0–99 Chart   179
0-99 Patterns (recording sheet)   180
Race for $1.00   181
Dollar Signs   182
Cover a Flat   183
0–99 Patterns   184
Number Puzzle   185
10-by-10 Grid   186
Fill the Cube   187
Make a Shape   188
Make a Shape Sample   189
Five Tower Game   190
Guess My Number   191
Play dollar bills   192

Bibliography   193

Index   195

INTRODUCTION

Developing understanding of place value is an important aspect of the math curriculum in the primary grades. As stated in the NCTM *Curriculum and Evaluation Standards for School Mathematics* (1989, page 39):

> Understanding place value is another critical step in the development of children's comprehension of number concepts. Prior to formal instruction on place value, the meanings children have for larger numbers are typically based on counting by ones and the "one more than" relationship between consecutive numbers. Since place-value meanings grow out of grouping experiences, counting knowledge should be integrated with meanings based on grouping. Children are then able to use and make sense of procedures for comparing, ordering, rounding, and operating with larger numbers.

Our place value system, which makes it possible for us to represent any number with the digits from 0 to 9, is not simple for children to understand. They need to be able to consider groups of 10 objects sometimes as individual objects and sometimes as groups of 10. They must learn that the value of each digit depends on its position in a number. Although most second graders know that 63 is larger than 36 because "63 comes after 36," not many notice, understand, or can verbalize the significance of the placement of the digits. The goal of this unit is to help children construct understanding of the 10s and 1s structure of our number system and learn to use their understanding when thinking about and working with numbers.

What's in the Unit

This unit on place value was created to respond to the current guidelines for mathematics instruction. In this five- to six-week unit, students are given a broad range of experiences to help them make sense of large numbers and develop understanding of our place value system. They are introduced to activities that approach place value in a variety of ways—estimating and counting large numbers of objects, looking for patterns in written numbers, relating our number system to money, working with concrete materials, and exploring numbers in everyday contexts. In general, students are engaged in activities that require them to compare the sizes of numbers and to think about the logic of their numerical representations.

During the unit, children participate in whole class lessons, work cooperatively in pairs, and do individual assignments. Writing is an integral part of their math learning. Children's books are incorporated into lessons. Homework is used to further students' classroom experiences as well as to communicate with parents about their children's learning.

All of the children in the class do the same activities. The activities are designed to be accessible for students with limited experience and understanding while, at the same time, to be of interest and value to students with more experience and deeper understanding. Throughout the unit, students are helped to develop understanding from interactions with the teacher, conversations with other students, opportunities to work with concrete materials, and problems that make them think about numbers.

The Structure of This Book

A challenge of teaching is to find activities that capture children's imaginations, give them access to a mathematical idea such as place value, and allow them to construct their own understanding of that idea. Not all children respond with the same interest to the same activities or learn equally well from them. Because of this, the unit provides a range of activities to help children find their own ways to learn.

The directions for instruction in this unit are organized into five components: *Whole Class Lessons, Menu Activities, Assessment, Children's Books,* and *Homework.* Also included in the unit are blackline masters for all menu activities and recording sheets and a bibliography.

Whole Class Lessons

Four whole class lessons, each requiring two to five class periods, give the class a common set of experiences on which to build their learning about place value. Two of the lessons should be taught at the beginning of the unit. One introduces children to the patterns on the 0–99 chart, and the other has children investigate the number of stars they can draw in one minute. The third activity uses interlocking cubes to help children connect the structure of numbers to a concrete material. The fourth lesson uses a children's book to help students investigate different ways to group and count.

The instructional directions for each lesson are presented in four sections:

Overview gives a brief description of the lesson.

Before the Lesson outlines the preparation needed before teaching the lesson.

Teaching Directions gives step-by-step instructions for presenting the lesson.

From the Classroom describes what happened when the lesson was taught to one class of second graders. The vignette helps bring alive the instructional guidelines by giving an over-the-shoulder look into a classroom, telling how lessons were organized, how students reacted, and how the teacher responded. The vignettes are not standards of what "should" happen but a record of what did happen with 25 children.

Menu Activities

The menu is a collection of activities that children do independently, either in pairs or individually. The tasks on the menu give children a variety of experiences with place value but do not conceptually build on one another. They therefore are not meant to be done in any particular sequence. Rather, menu activities pose problems, set up situations, and ask questions that help students interact with the mathematics they're studying. Nine activities are included on this menu. Five require the children to work with partners; four are suitable for individuals.

The instructional directions for each menu activity are presented in five sections:

Overview gives a brief description of the activity.

Before the Lesson outlines the preparation needed before the activity is introduced.

Getting Started gives instructions for introducing the activity.

From the Classroom describes what happened when the activity was introduced to one class of second graders. As with the *Whole Class Lessons,* the vignette gives a view into an actual classroom, describing how the teacher gave directions and how the students responded.

Linking Assessment with Instruction describes actual conversations with students that were useful for assessing their understanding. These vignettes model the kinds of interactions that are valuable for ongoing assessment.

For additional information about the menu system, see the introduction to the *Menu Activities* section that begins on page 83.

Assessment

Each unit suggests three general methods for assessing what children understand: informal assessments, on-demand assessments, and informal interviews. The *From the Classroom* and *Linking Assessment with Instruction* sections provide suggestions for informal assessments in the context of classroom instruction. The unit offers four on-demand assessments, two evolving from whole class lessons and two from menu activities. These assessments are listed in the Table of Contents and placed in the unit near the activities

from which they draw (identified by gray bars in the margins). Guidelines for individual interviews are given throughout the unit.

For specific information about assessing understanding, see the introduction to Assessment on page 13.

Children's Books

Children's books can be a motivating way to engage children in mathematical thinking and reasoning. They also provide a way to integrate literature with math instruction. For this unit, we recommend three children's books, each of which offers a way to enhance a lesson and give children additional support for thinking about large numbers and place value. The Children's Books section includes a synopsis of each book. A classroom vignette is provided for teaching the lesson or activity that uses the book.

Homework

Homework assignments have two purposes: They extend the work children are doing in class, and they inform parents about the instruction their children are getting. Suggestions for homework assignments and ways to communicate with parents are included in the Homework section.

Blackline Masters

Blackline masters for all menu activities are provided, along with blackline masters for recording sheets.

Bibliography

A bibliography of all resources cited in the book is included at the end of the book.

Important Classroom Issues

Setting the Stage for Cooperation

Throughout much of the unit, students are asked to work cooperatively with a partner. Interaction is an important ingredient for children's intellectual development. They learn from interaction with one another as well as with adults.

Teachers who have taught the unit have reported different systems for organizing children to work cooperatively. Some put pairs of numbers in a bag and have children draw to choose partners. Some assign partners. Some have seatmates work together. Others let children pick their own partners.

Some teachers have students work with the same partner for the entire unit. Others let children choose partners for each activity, allowing them either to change frequently or stay with the same person. Some don't have children work with specific partners but instead with the others who have chosen the same activity.

The system for organizing children matters less than the underlying classroom attitude. What's important is that children are encouraged to work together, listen to one another's ideas, and be willing to help classmates. Students should see their classroom as a place where cooperation and collaboration are valued and expected. This does not mean, of course, that children are never expected to work individually. However, it does respect the principle that interaction fosters learning and, therefore, that cooperation is basic to the culture of the classroom.

A System for the Menu Activities

Teachers report different ways for organizing the menu activities. Some teachers use a copy machine to enlarge the blackline masters of the menu tasks onto 11-by-17-inch paper, mount them on construction paper or tagboard, and post them. Although children are introduced orally to each activity, later they can refer to the directions for clarification. (Note: A set of posters with the menu activities is available for purchase from Cuisenaire Company of America.) When students need materials, they take them from the general supply and return them when they finish their work or at the end of class.

Rather than enlarge and post the tasks, other teachers duplicate about a half dozen of each and make them available for children to take to their seats. Mounting them on tagboard makes the copies more durable. As described, children obtain materials and worksheets from the general supply and work at their own seats. Some teachers put the tasks in booklets, making one for either each child or each pair of students.

Some teachers prefer to assign different locations in the classroom for different tasks. For each activity, they place a copy of the task and the worksheets and materials needed in a cardboard carton or rubber tub. At the beginning of menu time, they ask monitors to distribute the tubs to the locations. The number of chairs at each location determines the number of children that can work there.

Each of these systems encourages children to be independent and responsible for their learning. They are allowed to spend the amount of time needed on any one task and to make choices about the sequence in which they work on tasks. Also, the tasks are designed for children to do over and over again, avoiding the situation where a child is "finished" and has nothing to do.

How Children Record

Teachers also use different procedures to organize the way children record their learning. Some prepare folders for each child, either by folding 12-by-18-inch construction paper or by using regular file folders, and require children to record individually even when working cooperatively. Some teachers prepare folders for partners and have the partners collaborate on their written work. Other teachers don't use folders but have students place their finished work in an "In" basket.

Some teachers have children copy the list of menu activities and keep track of what they do by putting a check by an activity each time they do it.

Other teachers give children a list of the menu activities by duplicating the blackline master on page 178. It's important that the recording system is clear to the class and helps the teacher keep track of children's progress.

About Writing in Math Class

For both learning activities and assessments, teachers must rely on children's writing to get insights into their thinking. Helping children learn to describe their reasoning processes, and become comfortable doing so, is extremely important and requires planning and attention. Experience and encouragement are two major ingredients.

I often remind students that their writing is important because it helps me learn about how they are thinking, which helps me become a better teacher. I reinforce, over and over again, that I am the audience for their writing and that they need to provide me with sufficient details to help me understand their thinking and reasoning processes.

When children are writing solutions to problems, I circulate, offer encouragement, and often push for more. Usually when children think their papers are complete, I think they still need revision. "That's a good beginning," I say if they've explained their thinking incompletely. "Use words," I say if they've used only numbers and pictures. "Include numbers," I say, if they used only words and pictures. "Write some more," I say if their explanation is skimpy and lacks detail.

As often as possible in the bustle of classroom work, I have individual children read their papers aloud to me, and I make suggestions for revisions. At times, I point out that they need periods or capital letters at the beginning of sentences and correct their spelling; at other times, I let errors pass. These sorts of decisions fall in the realm of the art and craft of teaching, and I tailor my decisions to the individual children and to the assignment. I find that, over time, children come to accept revising and editing of their math writing as part of their process of learning.

In general, I push and push (as in nag and nag), respecting, of course, individual children's differences. And at all times my message to children is consistent: Write only what makes sense to you, and persist until it does. Getting students to express their ideas in writing never gets easy in the classroom, but it gets easier as the year progresses. And it's worth the effort for the payoff both to students' learning and teachers' assessments.

Managing Materials and Supplies

Teachers who have taught this unit gave children time to explore the concrete materials they needed to use. Most teachers devoted several weeks at the beginning of the school year to free exploration of materials. Also, all teachers gave students guidelines for the care and storage of materials.

Materials

The following materials and supplies are needed for the Place Value unit:
- Dice, about one pair per child
- Color Tiles (1-inch square tiles in four colors), one set of 400
- Base Ten Blocks (sets of at least 30 unit cubes, 20 tens rods, and 2 hundreds squares for each pair of children), six sets

■ Interlocking cubes (Multilink, Snap, or Unifix cubes, 3/4-inch on a side), 100
■ Hundreds Number Wall Chart, a 10-by-10 chart of transparent plastic pockets and cards for the numbers from 0 to 100, one for the class-room
■ If there is no sweep second hand on your class clock, timers or stop-watches to time one minute, six
■ Bucket, bowl, or other container large enough to hold 100 interlock-ing cubes
■ 1-quart ziploc-style baggies, each with 30 pennies, 20 dimes, and 2 play dollars, at least six
■ 1-quart zip-top baggies, each half-filled with popcorn, at least six
■ 1-quart zip-top baggies, each half-filled with lentils, at least six

General Classroom Supplies

■ 3-by-3-inch Post-it™ Notes, at least one packet
■ Ample supplies of paper, including large sheets of newsprint or chart paper and construction paper
■ Letter-size envelopes, one per child, plus several extras
■ A shoebox-size box
■ Scissors, at least one for each pair of children
■ Glue
■ Tape

In addition, recording sheets specified for individual activities are included in the Blackline Masters section. Most teachers choose to have supplies of each sheet available for children to take when needed. Also, see the Children's Books section for information about the children's books that have been integrated into this unit.

A Comment about Calculators

It's assumed that during this unit, and in the classroom throughout the year, calculators are as available to the children as pencils, paper, rulers, and other general classroom supplies. You may occasionally ask students not to use calculators if you want to know about their ability to deal with numbers on their own. However, such times should be the exception rather than the rule. Children should regard calculators as tools that are generally available for their use when doing mathematics.

As with other materials, children need time to become familiar with cal-culators. Some children will find them fascinating and useful; others will not be interested in or comfortable with them.

A Suggested Daily Schedule

It's helpful to think through the entire unit and make an overall teaching plan. However, it isn't possible to predict how a class will respond as the unit progresses, and adjustments and changes will most likely have to be

made. The following day-to-day schedule is a suggested guide. It offers a plan that varies the pace of daily instruction, interweaving days for whole class lessons with days for independent work on menu activities, and mixing in reading children's books and whole class discussions.

Day 1   Whole Class Lesson: The 0–99 Chart, Part 1

Put the numbers from 0 to 15 on the chart and have students place others.

Day 2   Whole Class Lesson: The 0–99 Chart, Part 1 (continued)
Assessment: Numbers on the 0–99 Chart

Begin by having the class count the number of cards on the chart. After 12 to 15 children place additional number cards, remove the chart (so children can't count) and have students do the assessment: *Numbers on the 0–99 Chart*.

Day 3   Whole Class Lesson: Stars in One Minute, Part 1

Draw stars while the children time one minute. Count them in several ways, including by 2s, 5s, and 10s. If there is time, read *Draw Me a Star* by Eric Carle.

Day 4   Whole Class Lesson: Stars in One Minute, Part 2

If you didn't read *Draw Me a Star* on Day 3, do so at the beginning of the lesson. Give the children time to practice making stars and continue with Part 2 of the lesson, having the children draw stars while you time one minute. If there is time, have students place additional number cards on the 0–99 chart.

Day 5   Whole Class Lesson: Stars in One Minute, Part 3

Children again draw stars for one minute, count them, and record on Post-It™ Notes. Organize their data into a class graph. If there is time, continue having students place additional number cards on the 0–99 chart. Give homework assignment: *Stars in One Minute*.

Day 6   Introduce Three Menu Activities: Race for $1.00, Dollar Signs, Cover a Flat

Start class by having children record data from *Stars in One Minute* homework. Add the data to the class graph or make a new graph. Tell children who did not bring the information to do so the next day. Then present the directions for the three menu activities, inviting students to help model each. For the remainder of the period, students choose an activity from the menu.

Day 7   Menu

If the 0–99 chart has not been filled in completely, have students place the remaining cards. Also, if additional children bring *Stars in One Minute* data from home, add the data to the class graph. Use the bulk of the period for students to choose and work on activities from the menu.

Day 8   **Whole Class Lesson: The 0–99 Chart, Part 2**

Investigate patterns on the 0–99 chart and ask several students to present their rules for others to guess.

Day 9   **Menu**

Begin class with a few students presenting the rules for their 0–99 chart patterns. Then students choose and work on activities from the menu.

Day 10   **Introduce Menu Activity: 0–99 Patterns**

After introducing *0–99 Patterns,* have the class continue choosing and working on activities from the menu. This is a possible day to interrupt the menu early and read aloud *The Go-Around Dollar.* Give homework assignment: *Race for $1.00.*

Day 11   **Introduce Menu Activity: Number Puzzle**

Begin class by having children report their experiences at home playing *Race for $1.00.* Then show the students how to make number puzzles. It will take most children the entire class period to make their puzzles; those who finish early can choose and work on an activity from the menu.

Day 12   **Menu**

Students who didn't finish their puzzles the day before should finish them first before choosing and working on an activity from the menu. If you haven't read *The Go-Around Dollar,* stop menu work early to do so.

Day 13   **Whole Class Lesson: Counting Fish**

Have each child put two interlocking cubes into a bucket or bowl. Ask children to figure out how many fish are in the bowl, record their answers, and explain their reasoning. As children finish and you accept their work, have them choose a menu activity.

Day 14   **Whole Class Lesson: Counting Fish (continued)**

Begin class by having several children present their work to share how they counted the fish. Then count the cubes, grouping them by 2s, 5s, and 10s.

Day 15   **Assessment: How Many 10s?**

The children write about the number of 10s and 1s there are in the total number of fish in the bowl. As children finish and you accept their work, have them choose a menu activity. Give homework assignment: *Dollar Signs.*

Day 16   **Introduce Two Menu Activities: Fill the Cube, Make a Shape**

Begin class by having children report their experiences at home doing *Dollar Signs.* Introduce *Fill the Cube* and *Make a Shape,* and then have students choose and work on activities from the menu.

Day 17   **Menu**

Review directions for *Fill the Cube* and *Make a Shape* and have students choose and work on activities from the menu.

Day 18   **Whole Class Lesson: Stars in One Minute, Part 3 (continued)**
                Menu

Focus the class on the *Stars in One Minute* graph and process the data by asking students to make generalizations. Record about six statements on chart paper. Spread this activity over two days, using the second half of each period for menu work.

Day 19   **Whole Class Lesson: Stars in One Minute, Part 3 (continued)**
                Menu

Continue with more student generalizations for the *Stars in One Minute* graph. Use the second half of the period to explain and organize the *Number Puzzle* homework assignment. Have children collect their puzzles (the puzzle box may need some sorting out, as puzzle pieces can get lost) and prepare a new chart to take home. Give homework assignment: *Number Puzzle.*

Day 20   **Introduce Two Menu Activities: Five Tower Game,**
                Guess My Number

Begin class by asking children to report their experiences at home with *Number Puzzles.* Return the children's puzzles to the puzzle box and have them add the ones they made at home. Then introduce *Five Tower Game* and *Guess My Number,* and let students choose and work on activities from the menu.

Day 21   **Menu**

Begin class with a discussion of students' menu work, asking them to tell about their favorite activities. You may want to show them some student work from their folders that models the kind of work you'd like all of them to do. Then let them choose and work on activities from the menu.

Day 22   **Assessment: Catherine's Problem**

Present the assessment problem. Students who finish early can choose and work on menu activities. Give homework assignment: *Guess My Number.*

Day 23   **Whole Class Lesson: The King's Commissioners**

Begin class by having children report their experiences at home playing *Guess My Number.* Then read *The King's Commissioners.* Discuss and have children describe in writing the counting systems.

Day 24   **Whole Class Lesson: The King's Commissioners (continued)**

Return to *The King's Commissioners* story. Ask students to think about other commissioners the King might appoint and how many he might need. Present optional writing assignment. Children can work on optional assignment or choose activities from the menu.

Day 25   Assessment: How Much Is Covered?

Present the assessment problem. Students who finish early can choose and work on activities from the menu. If you'd like, take time to have students organize their folders, discarding papers that aren't needed.

A Letter to Parents

Although parents learn about their children's experiences from homework assignments and papers sent home, you may want to give them general information about the unit before you begin teaching it. The following is a sample letter that informs parents about the goals of the unit and introduces them to some of the activities their children will be doing.

Dear Parent,

We are about to begin work on a math unit that focuses on place value and estimation. Our place value system allows us to represent any number with just ten digits—0, 1, 2, 3, 4, 5, 6, 7, 8, and 9. Children need many experiences relating large quantities of objects to their numerical representations in order to learn about how our place value system works. They must learn that symbols have different values, depending on their positions in numbers, and what those values are. The difference between the value of the 3s in 36 and 63, although obvious to adults, is not always obvious to children.

To help children develop an understanding of place value, this unit provides work with a variety of concrete materials. Children experience estimating and counting large numbers of things—popcorn, tiles, stars they draw, etc. They examine patterns on the 0–99 chart. They learn a game in which they use dimes and pennies to make a dollar, thus relating our number system to money. They also learn to play a guessing game that requires them to compare the sizes of numbers up to 100.

While the activities focus on estimation and large numbers, they also provide children experience with ideas in the strands of measurement, geometry, patterns, logical reasoning, and statistics.

From time to time, the children will have the assignment to teach someone at home one of the activities or games they have learned in class. These homework assignments will give you firsthand experience with the unit.

If you have any questions, please do not hesitate to call.

Sincerely,

A Final Comment

The decisions teachers make every day in the classroom are the heart of teaching. Although this book attempts to provide clear and detailed information about lessons and activities, it isn't a recipe that can be followed step-by-step. Rather, the book offers options that require teachers to make decisions in several areas: sequencing activities, organizing the classroom, grouping children, communicating with parents, and dealing with the needs of individual children. Keep in mind that there is no "best" or "right" way to teach the unit. The aim is to engage children in mathematical investigations, to inspire them to think and reason, and to enable them to enjoy their learning.

CONTENTS

Individual Interviews   17
Numbers on the 0–99 Chart   36
How Many 10s?   67
How Much Is Covered?   116
Catherine's Problem   140

ASSESSMENTS

Assessing children's understanding is an ongoing process. In the classroom, teachers learn about what students know from listening to what they say during class discussions, observing and listening as they work on independent activities, conversing with individual children, and reading their written work. From these observations and interactions, teachers gain insights into children's thinking and reasoning processes and information about children's mathematical interests and abilities.

Place value plays an important part in the primary mathematics curriculum. The topic is a complex one that deserves careful and specific scrutiny. Children's learning, however, is not isolated into separate topics. Throughout the unit, for example, children express their ideas orally and in writing and, therefore, their language skills are integral to their math learning. Some of the activities in the unit involve the children with other topics in the mathematics curriculum, including graphing and interpreting data and measuring time.

For these reasons, it's important to remember that children's mathematical understanding is best assessed in the context of their learning in general. However, because this unit focuses specifically on helping children learn about the place value structure of our number system, this section on assessment primarily addresses students' understanding in that area. The section offers suggestions to help teachers make assessment an ongoing part of instruction in order to uncover and evaluate students' emerging understandings.

Also, children's developmental levels have a direct impact on their ability to understand place value. Although young children can count 16 objects, they don't necessarily see that 16 is the same as one group of 10 and 6 extras. They understand how to count individual objects, but they might not be able to count groups of objects in the same way. Children need

time to mature and experiences to draw upon in order to construct their own understanding about how our number system works.

What Does It Mean to Understand Place Value?

Most children at this age are familiar with numbers up to 100. They can count correctly, although some get confused when changing from one decade to the next—from 29 to 30 or 39 to 40, for example. They can write the numbers from 1 to 100, even though some from time to time still write individual digits backwards or reverse the digits in numerals. They can compare numbers—56 and 37, for example—and tell which is greater and which is less, even though they might not be able to explain why.

However, even with this familiarity, most children have not thought about how place value makes it possible to express all numbers with only the digits from 0 to 9. The goal of this unit is to help children develop an understanding of the 10s and 1s structure of our number system and the ability to use their understanding when thinking about and working with numbers.

The following three components are important indicators of children's understanding of place value. These are not separate or sequential aspects of place value but overlapping ideas that together contribute to children's overall understanding.

The Relationship Between Numbers and Groups of 10s and 1s

Children who have some understanding of the relationship between numbers and groups of 10s and 1s know that if they have three groups of 10 objects and seven extras, they have 37 objects altogether. Also, if they have 42 objects, they know they can make four groups of 10 and have two extras.

The Significance of the Positions of Digits in Numbers

When children have learned the significance of the placement of digits in numbers, they can explain the meaning of each digit. For example, when asked about the "3" and the "6" in 36, they know that the "6" stands for six individual units and the "3" stands for three groups of 10.

Solving Addition Problems

Children who understand place value can make use of the 10s and 1s structure of numbers to do addition, with and without regrouping. (Children who do not yet have a firm understanding of place value will rely on counting in some way.) In traditional instructional programs, place value is taught before addition as a prerequisite for learning to add with regrouping. Also, traditional instruction sees teaching of the standard algorithm—"carrying" or "regrouping"—as an important aspect of mathematics instruction in the primary grades. However, this unit takes the approach that integrating addition and regrouping with place value helps children see the relationship between the two ideas in a natural way. The unit doesn't "teach" students how to regroup but presents problems that require combining numbers to reach solutions. The emphasis isn't on procedures for adding but rather on the problem to be solved. From children's solutions, teachers can assess their ability to make use of the place value structure of our number system when working with numbers.

Assessment in the Classroom

There is no one "right" or "best" way to assess student understanding in classroom settings. Rather, teachers must take an eclectic approach, finding ways to integrate assessment into instruction in as many ways as possible. In all assessments, teachers pose questions and tasks to stimulate students' thinking, listen to their ideas, and ask them to clarify and justify their ideas orally and in writing.

Three categories of assessments are suggested in the unit:

Linking Assessment with Instruction refers to assessments that are conducted during the course of whole class lessons or menu activities. They are often incidental and always responsive to the situation at hand.

On-Demand Assessment Tasks are specific assignments that teachers structure to learn about students. Examining children's responses to on-demand assessments gives a reading on how the class in general is responding and what individual children know.

Individual Interviews provide in-depth information about children. Although interviews are extremely valuable for close scrutiny of a student's thinking, they're difficult to conduct during classroom instruction.

Following is information about each of these assessment categories.

Linking Assessment with Instruction

The most natural way to collect information about what students understand is to do so during the regular course of classroom instruction, both in whole class discussions and when the students are working individually or in pairs on menu activities or other assignments.

In whole class discussions, a general guideline is to encourage students at all times to explain their thinking processes. As often as possible, ask questions that require children to explain their thinking, rather than merely provide a correct answer. If you do ask a question that children can answer with "yes," "no," or a single numerical answer, probe further and ask them to elaborate by giving prompts such as: "Why do you think that?," "Explain why," or "Try and convince us." It's extremely important to question children even when they give correct responses. That way, not only do their explanations reveal the thinking and reasoning that underlie their solutions, but students learn that their thinking and reasoning, not merely quick and correct responses, are important and valued. For the students responding, explaining their thinking helps them cement and extend their learning; for the others, hearing others' ideas provides them with different points of view.

Observing students at work on menu activities is another way to assess their understanding. At times, it's best not to interrupt but merely to listen to learn how they are thinking about an activity. At other times, it's helpful to ask questions, pose new problems, or just have students explain what they're doing. It's possible to gain valuable information about students during these informal, and often incidental, interactions.

From the Classroom sections in all whole class lessons and menu activities provide examples of informal assessments conducted during whole class discussions. Such assessments can occur either while an activity is introduced or during a later class discussion. In addition, menu activities include *Linking Assessment with Instruction* sections that describe informal

assessments when children are working on menu activities. While the identical situations described in these sections won't arise in other classroom situations, the vignettes provide prototypes for the kinds of discussions that are possible during menu time.

Providing On-Demand Assessment Tasks
An on-demand assessment task is a kind of quiz. However, for the children, it isn't apparent that an on-demand assessment is a testing situation. Rather, it's another activity, like others they've been engaged with during the unit, that presents them with a situation that requires them to think, reason, or reflect on an idea.

The on-demand assessments suggested in this unit are extensions of the whole class lessons or menu activities. This is done so that the problems occur in contexts with which the students are familiar. Because the assessments relate to the specific situations that occurred in the class described, they will have to be altered in other classes. However, the assessment descriptions explain their underlying goals and suggest ways to adapt them for other classroom situations. They therefore offer prototypes of the kinds of problems that are useful for assessing children's understanding.

For on-demand assessments, it's necessary to rely on children's writing to get insights into their thinking. See the *About Writing in Math Class* section on page 6 for ways to help children learn to write and become comfortable doing so.

All the assessments listed in the contents are on-demand assessments. They are placed throughout the unit, each following the whole class lesson or menu activity it extends.

Conducting Individual Interviews
With all the demands of classroom instruction, teachers have little time to conduct in-depth interviews with students. When possible, however, it's valuable for teachers to make time for individual assessments with some children, possibly during quiet reading time, recess, or when the rest of the class goes to the library. Conducting even a few interviews can strengthen teachers' questioning skills and is useful preparation for talking with students in more active class settings.

The section *Individual Interviews* describes the assessments I did with some of my second graders. The questions in these interviews are based on the guidelines in the *What Does It Mean to Understand Place Value?* section above. Note: Part 1 of the videotape series *Mathematics: Assessing Understanding* shows individual interviews with five children, ages seven through nine, and focuses on their number sense and understanding of place value. (For information, see the Bibliography on page 193.)

ASSESSMENT Individual Interviews

One-on-one interviews, while the least practical for classroom teachers, are the most effective for revealing a child's understanding of place value. This section presents questions that are useful for finding out what students know and don't know about place value. Although it's not possible during classroom instruction to conduct individual interviews, interviewing even a few students can help hone teachers' skills at questioning children during regular lessons. For these interviews, choosing children who represent a range of experience and understanding is useful for getting a sense of the breadth of reactions and responses students will have about place value.

When conducting individual interviews, it's important to suggest, prod, push, question, and encourage. When students give responses, ask them to explain their thinking: "Why do you think that?" "Why does that make sense to you?" "Can you explain that?" If children change their minds at any time, probe their thinking: "Why does your new idea make sense?" "How come you changed your thinking?" If children give an incorrect response, present them with contradictory information and ask them to reconsider their thinking in light of the new information.

However, it's also important to avoid leading the children and directing them to think in any particular way. The goal for individual interviews is the same as for all lessons and assessments—to have children express their own ideas and explain their understanding in ways that make sense to them. At all times, the focus should be on finding out how they think and reason. The following sequence of questions is useful for a 10- to 15-minute interview to assess children's understanding of place value.

NOTE Throughout interviews, it's just as essential to question children when they give correct responses as when they give incorrect responses. Do not be seduced by quick, right answers as indicators of understanding, but push for explanations that reveal understanding.

1. The Relationship Between Numbers and Groups of 10s and 1s

Give children a cup with 24 tiles or beans and direct them to put the objects into groups of 10. Ask: *How many groups of 10 and how many extras are there?* Then ask: *How many are there in all?* Finally, have the children write the number.

All students should be able to put the tiles or beans into groups of 10 and report the number of groups and extras. However, students' responses to telling the total number of tiles or beans will differ. Those children who fully understand place value will know immediately that there are 24 beans or tiles; those whose understanding is partial or fragile may have to combine the 10s and add on the extras; some children will have to count the tiles or beans one by one.

2. The Significance of the Positions of Digits in Numbers

Present a problem that gives insights into children's number sense while also generating a number different from 24. Ask: *Suppose I didn't want 24 tiles but only 16. Take some away so that only 16 are left.* Subtraction is hard for primary children. While some children can figure out how many tiles to remove, others will need to count out 16 tiles and discard the rest.

Have the children write 16 and then point to the 6 in the numeral and ask: *Can you show with the tiles what the 6 means?* Then point to the 1 and ask: *Can you show with the tiles what the 1 means?* (Note: This question was developed by Constance Kamii and is included in her article "Encouraging Thinking in Mathematics." See the Bibliography, page 193.)

Children who understand place value show 6 tiles for the 6 and then explain that the 1 represents the remaining 10 tiles. However, if children show, as is typical with second graders, that the 1 means one tile, probe further: *If these six tiles stand for the 6 and this one tile is the 1, then where do the rest of the tiles belong?* This prompt is designed to present students with a contradiction and to provide another way to interpret their understanding.

3. Solving an Addition Problem

Give the children an addition problem and check again on their understanding of the meaning of the digits in a number. Ask: *Suppose you took 25 more tiles. How would you figure out how many you would have altogether?* Children who understand place value will have some way of using their information about 10s and 1s to solve the problem. If the problem is too difficult, children will respond that they have to get tiles and count them or will count on their fingers. If so, change the problem to a simpler one that requires less counting: *If you add 5 more tiles onto the 16, how many will you have?*

Most children will count on from 16 to 21 using tiles, on their fingers, or in their head; some will take five tiles and count them all, starting with 1. When children answer either problem, have them verify their calculation with the tiles. If they were incorrect, they'll have the chance to deal with the inconsistency between their idea and what the tiles show.

Ask: *If you put all those tiles into groups of 10, how many groups would you have? Would there be any extras?* Children who understand place value will be able to give the information easily; children whose understanding is partial or fragile may be able to answer the question after thinking about the numbers and doing some figuring; some children will have no idea and no way to think about the question.

If you'd like, have children write the number and ask the same questions recommended above for the number 16, asking them to interpret the meaning of the digits in the numeral. Some children can apply the structure of 10s and 1s to the meaning of the digits in numbers 20 and larger, while the structure doesn't make sense for numbers in the teens.

Note: Part 1 of the videotape series *Mathematics: Assessing Understanding* shows individual interviews with five children, ages seven through nine, and focuses on their number sense and understanding of the place value structure of our number system. The interviews on the tapes include some of the questions presented above, and some others as well. (For information, see the Bibliography, page 193.)

FROM THE CLASSROOM

There was a range of responses from the interviews I conducted with second graders in my class. Andrew, for example, answered all the questions confidently and correctly. After he put the tiles into two groups of 10 with four extras, he knew that there were 24 tiles in the cup. When I asked him how he knew this, he responded quickly, "There are two 10s and that's 20, and four more make 24."

When I asked Andrew to remove some tiles to leave just 16, he thought for a moment and then said, "I'll take away four and then four."

"Why does that make sense?" I probed.

"Because 4 gets me down to 20 and then 4 more gets me down to 16," he answered.

Andrew wrote the number and correctly identified that the 6 represented 6 tiles and the 1 stood for the 10 that were left. "It tells how many 10s you have," he said to explain.

He was able to add 16 and 25 in his head. "You have 30," he said, combining the 10 from 16 and the 20 from 25, "and then you put one from the 6 on the 5 and that makes another 10 so you have 40, and then you add the extra on, so it's 41." When I asked Andrew how many 10s and 1s there were in 41, he easily answered that there were four 10s and one extra.

Only two children in my class demonstrated this degree of confidence and knowledge. Most students' responses showed they had only partial understanding. For example, when Seth put the tiles into two groups of 10 with four extras, he reported easily and confidently that there were 24 altogether. He struggled, however, to take some away to be left with 16, using a trial-and-error method of removing some, counting, and adjusting until he was correct.

When explaining the digits in 16, Seth showed six tiles for the 6 and one tile for the 1.

"What about these tiles?" I asked, pointing to the nine tiles left over. "Where are these shown in the number?" He just shrugged.

When I asked Seth how he would add 25 more tiles, he said it would be hard to count that many. "Can I use paper?" he asked. Seth was used to drawing tally marks or writing a sequence of numbers to count on.

"Can you figure out how many tiles you would have if you added just five more?" I asked. Seth nodded and counted on his fingers to get 21. Seth verified his answer with the tiles and wrote the number easily.

I then asked, "How many groups of 10s and extras do you think there are with those 21 tiles?" Seth answered correctly that there were two 10s and one extra. When I asked him to show me with the tiles what the 1 and the 2 meant, however, he responded in the same way he had with 16, showing me one tile for the 1 and two tiles for the 2.

Leslie gave some different responses. She knew easily that there were 24 tiles in the cup and could explain her reasoning. She couldn't figure out how many to remove to get 16, however, and counted out 16 tiles, moving the rest aside.

Leslie answered incorrectly, as Seth did, when explaining the meaning of the digits in 16. But, with the number 21, she answered that the 1 meant one tile and the 2 meant the two 10s. I then had Leslie count out 15 tiles and write the numeral. I asked the same question. She showed me

five tiles for the 5 and then one tile for the 10. "No, wait a minute," she said, "that can't be right. It should be 10. But I don't know if I have enough to make a 10." It wasn't obvious to Leslie that if she took 5 tiles from 15, 10 would be left; she had to count the tiles to find out.

As I interviewed the children, I was amazed at the variations in their thinking. It seemed that each had different bits and pieces of understanding. They all could arrange the 24 tiles into two groups of 10 with four extras. All but three answered easily that there were 24 tiles and could explain their thinking; the three others had to count the tiles one by one. All of the children knew how to write the number 24.

Of the 26 students in the class, all but four of the children solved the problem of taking away some tiles from the 24 to get 16 by counting a pile of 16 and discarding the rest. This didn't surprise me; subtraction is difficult for children this age. All of the children were able to write the number 16, but only six of them correctly identified the meaning of the 6 and the 1. I was surprised that Eli and Gwyn answered correctly, as I wouldn't have surmised they would from my contact with them during regular class work.

Five children were able to solve the harder problem of adding 25 and 16 in a way that showed use of 10s and 1s. All of them thought about the 10s first and then dealt with the 1s. All but two children could add 5 to 16 by counting on.

When I asked children how many groups of 10s and extras there were in their new number, either 41 or 21, about two-thirds of the class answered correctly. Half of those, however, when I asked about the meaning of the digits, didn't identify the 4 or 2 as representing groups of 10, but as individual tiles.

Molly was one of the children who knew that with 21 tiles, there would be two groups of 10 and one extra. "It would be like two bundles of sticks with 10 in each bundle," she said, "and then one extra stick not in a bundle. I did this in first grade."

Previously, however, Molly had said that the 1 in 16 was just one tile. I asked her about 16 again. "If you grouped 16 tiles into tens and extras," I asked, "what would happen?"

"You'd just have one big pile," she said. After thinking a moment, she revised her idea. "Well, you could make one bundle and then have some left over. But you don't need to because there are only 16." It's common for children not to apply their understanding of place value to numbers in the teens.

"If you did make a bundle," I probed, "how many extras would there be?"

"Oooh, that's hard," she said. "Wait a minute." I waited and she counted on her fingers. "I think it's 6," she said. Molly's response was similar to Leslie's response about the number 15.

My individual interviews reminded me that partial understanding and confusion are natural parts of the learning process. The children's assortment of responses reminded me that children learn in different and individual ways. I know that it's difficult for a classroom teacher to find time to do interviews with all children as I've described, but I strongly recommend doing some to have first-hand experience with finding out, in-depth, what children understand.

CONTENTS

The 0–99 Chart   22
Stars in One Minute   41
Counting Fish   56
The King's Commisioners   72

WHOLE CLASS LESSONS

The Place Value unit includes four whole class lessons, each requiring two to five class periods. Each provides experience with our place value system of numbers from a different perspective while preparing children for several independent menu activities.

The first lesson, *The 0–99 Chart*, focuses on the array of numbers on a 0–99 chart. There are two parts to the lesson.

The second lesson, *Stars in One Minute,* uses drawing and counting stars as the context for introducing children to different ways of counting large numbers of objects. The lesson is divided into three parts.

The third whole class lesson, *Counting Fish*, also presents children with the problem of counting a large number of objects. This lesson uses interlocking cubes to help children connect the 10s and 1s structure of our number system to a concrete material. *Counting Fish* offers a structure that can be repeated in other contexts; suggestions for variations are included.

The children's book *The King's Commissioners* provides the context for the fourth whole class lesson. In the story, 47 commissioners are counted in three different ways. Students explore why each way makes sense.

Each lesson has several parts and requires at least two class periods. It isn't necessary to present the separate parts on consecutive days. Also, it isn't necessary to teach all four lessons at the start of the unit before the menu activities are presented. Pacing should accommodate children's interest levels and your planning preferences. It's actually better to introduce some menu activities early in the unit so that during whole class lessons, when children typically finish work at different times, they will have some options for staying meaningfully engaged mathematically. (See A Suggested Daily Schedule on pages 7–11 for one possible day-by-day plan.)

WHOLE CLASS LESSON   The 0–99 Chart

Overview

The whole class lesson, *The 0–99 Chart*, begins the unit by focusing the students on an orderly arrangement of the numbers from 0 to 99. Although most children at this age are familiar with numbers up to 100, most of them haven't thought about the 10s and 1s structure of our number system or examined patterns that emerge from looking at the numbers in an organized array. The activities in this lesson invite students to examine numbers in a variety of ways. Also, the lesson provides children with a context for developing familiarity with words such as *digit, horizontal, vertical, diagonal, row,* and *column.*

Note: The first day of this lesson, taught to a different class of children than is described in this unit, appears on Part 1 of the videotape series *Mathematics: Teaching for Understanding.* (For information, see the Bibliography on page 193.)

Before the lesson

Gather these materials:
■ A hundred number wall chart with transparent plastic pockets that hold number cards from 0 to 99 (See the Bibliography on page 193.)
■ Blackline masters: 0–99 Chart and 0–99 Patterns, one or two per child (See Blackline Masters section, pages 179 and 180.)

Teaching directions

This lesson has two parts. Part 1 focuses children on locating numbers on the 0–99 chart and includes a suggestion for a whole class assessment to determine children's use of our place value system when adding numbers. In Part 2, children begin an investigation of patterns on the 0–99 chart and continue it through an independent menu activity. As described below, each part of the lesson requires several math periods, which can be spread over time or done sequentially. Part 1 is well suited for beginning the entire unit; Part 2 can be introduced later. (See A Suggested Daily Schedule on pages 8–9 for a day-by-day plan.)

Part 1: Building the 0–99 Chart
■ Insert the number cards from 0 to15 into the wall chart.

0	1	2	3	4	5	6	7	8	9
10	11	12	13	14	15				

Explain to the children that you'll show other number cards and ask for volunteers to figure out where they belong on the chart. You may wish to have children volunteer individually or work in pairs to locate the position of the cards. Do not choose numbers sequentially.

■ As children locate numbers on the chart, have them explain how they decided where to put them. If a child has difficulty explaining, choose a volunteer to help. To prompt students, say: "Convince the rest of the class that you've put the number in the proper place."

■ Continue having students add numbers to the chart over the next several days. Spreading the experience over a few class periods gives children time to reflect on the patterns that emerge in the chart.

■ You can use a partially filled chart as a beginning assessment of children's abilities to add numbers with regrouping. For a description, see the assessment on page 36.

Part 2: Investigating Patterns on the 0–99 Chart

■ Tell the children that you've thought of a rule that describes some of the numbers on the 0–99 chart, and they are to figure out which numbers fit the rule. Give the rule: *All the two-digit numbers on the chart that have both digits the same.*

■ Have children guess numbers. If they guess correctly, turn the number card to its blank side (Note: Children most likely won't know the meaning of the word "digit." Don't tell them, however; let them figure it out from the context of the activity.)

■ When all the numbers that fit the rule have been guessed—*11, 22, 33, 44, 55, 66, 77, 88,* and *99*—have children explain what they think the word "digit" means. Ask them to describe what the pattern looks like. Typically, children use phrases like "on a slant," "like a staircase," "on a diagonal," "from corner to corner," etc.

■ Ask the children to think of rules that are different from yours. Choose a student to come up and whisper a rule to you but not announce it to the class. Instead, have the student call on others to guess numbers that might fit the rule. When a guess is correct, turn over the card. The class tries to figure out the rule from the correct guesses. When all the appropriate cards have been turned over, have students describe what the pattern looks like.

■ After the class has guessed the rules of two or three children, give each child a copy of the 0–99 Patterns blackline master. (See page 180.) Each child writes his or her rule on the bottom half of the page and colors in the appropriate numbers on the chart at the top.

■ On the following days, you might want to ask more children to play *Guess My Rule* with the class. Also, use the student papers for the independent menu activity, *0–99 Patterns,* on page 122.

FROM THE CLASSROOM

Part 1: Locating Numbers on the 0–99 Chart

For this lesson, I used a commercial hundred wall chart and prepared by inserting the numbers from 0 to 15.

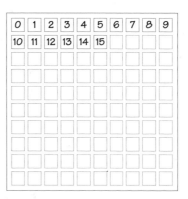

My plan was to show children other number cards, one by one, and have them figure out where they belonged on the chart. (Note: In previous years when I haven't had a commercial chart, I've ruled a 10-by-10 grid onto a large sheet of chart paper and filled in the numbers from 0 to 15. Then I'd write a number on the board and have a child come up and point to the space on the grid where it belonged. This method worked fine, but I found the investment in a commercial chart to be valuable, as it allows me more flexibility in my lessons.) "When I hold up a number card," I said to the class, "raise your hand if you'd like to come up and put it on the chart where it belongs." I held up the number 25 and about half the students raised their hands.

I called on Jonathan. When he came up to place the card, others shouted advice. "Further up." "Over there." "Oooh, it's easy." "I know, I know." "No, higher." I wasn't able to quiet them entirely. Jonathan kept his calm, but barely, carefully counted on from 15, keeping track of the spaces with his finger, and inserted the card correctly.

I called the class to attention. "We need to talk before we continue," I said. I talked to them about the inappropriateness of their behavior and also told them what they should be doing when one of their classmates is at the chart. "While someone else is thinking," I said, "you also should be thinking about where the number belongs. After someone places a card, then raise your hand if you disagree."

To reinforce my directions, I asked who understood what they were supposed to be doing when someone else was at the board. Several children raised their hands, and I had Gwyn explain.

"Remember," I concluded before returning to the activity, "you'll each have a turn."

I called on Catherine, and the class behaved well as she put up the card. Molly was next, and a few children called out. When Seth came up, however, the calling out escalated, and the atmosphere was more like a frantic TV quiz show than a classroom. I stopped the activity and talked again to the class, taking a different approach.

"I know you're excited," I said. "And I know you all have ideas about how to place the numbers. But you can't call out. Instead, try whispering to your partner when someone else is up at the chart."

I continued and called on Maria. The class was relatively quiet, although some of their comments were borderline whispers. When Katy came up, the calling out began again. Katy became completely flustered and broke out in tears. She jammed the number card into a slot and stormed to her seat.

"Uh, oh," Hassan said, "Katy's crying." The class quieted, suddenly sober and repentant.

I talked with them about the risk of coming to the front of the room and trying to figure out where a number belonged, how it seemed easy from their seats, but that being up at the front of the room was a different experience. I told them about the importance of taking risks to try out their thinking. I told them that they could help one another by giving each person time to think.

It took the calamity with Katy for the class to calm down. I'm amazed that even with 30 years of teaching experience, I still have times when all my managerial skills seem to vanish in a classroom situation. However, the 30 years of experience also help me keep my sights and not give up. The activity was valuable and enjoyable to the children. I was sorry Katy was hurt, but I'd have to wait until later to rethink how I might have dealt with the class differently.

I continued and the lesson went well. The excitement was still high, and I had to remind several children not to talk. But the improvement was enormous, and I was able to focus on the students' methods for placing numbers instead of on the behavior of the rest of the class. I noted which children located spaces by looking at patterns, locating the 7s column and the 30s row, for example, and which children had to start with a number already on the chart and count spaces to decide where a number belonged.

A Class Discussion

After each of the 23 children had placed a number on the chart, I led a class discussion around three questions:

1. How many numbers will be on the chart when it's all filled in?
2. If there are 39 numbers on the chart already, how many pockets are still empty?
3. Two numbers like 36 and 63 use the same two numbers, but they aren't the same amounts. Which is more and how do you know?

The first question sparked a lively discussion. Some children thought there would be 99 and some thought 100. Their reasons varied.

Teddy said, "I think there are 100 because the numbers go to 99 and you have to count the zero."

Molly said, "It only goes to 99 so there are 99. Zero doesn't count."

Seth said, "You can count the rows." He came up to the front of the room and pointed at the rows as he counted by 10s to 100.

"You can count the other way," Nick said. He came up and showed how to count the columns. "But I still think it's 99 because you don't have 100."

"Look," Marina said, "if you start with a 1, then you would get to 100."

"But you'd have to move them all," Hassan said.

"Do you have a 100 card?" Leslie asked.

I showed them the number card with 100 and asked where it would go.

"Next to the 99," Gwyn said, "but you need another pocket."

"No, under the 90," Rudy said.

"Suppose I started with 1 and rearranged the numbers on the chart," I said. "How would the chart look?"

The class got very quiet.

"You'd have to move them all," Teddy said.

"That would be a lot of work," Sarah said.

"You'd put the 100 on, but you wouldn't have room for the zero," Nick added.

"This is hard," Maria said.

"Are there any other ideas about how many numbers will be on the chart when it's all filled in?" I asked. There still was a difference of opinion and I dropped the issue, planning to come back to it after they had more experience with the chart and it was completely filled in.

Question number two about the number of empty pockets was too hard for all but about six of the children. I allowed them to offer their ideas and then went on to the third question. By this time, the children were getting tired, and only a few responded. Andrew gave a clear explanation of place value, pointing out the difference between 10s and 1s. A few others had ideas but weren't as articulate as Andrew.

The Following Day

The next day, I began class by having children put additional numbers on the 0–99 chart. I changed my method, however, and led the activity in silence, trying to diffuse the energy from the previous day. I explained to the children how we'd work.

"I'm going to draw a star on the board. I call it the 'Silent Star' and no one is allowed to talk until I erase it. Even I'm not allowed to talk, so we'll do everything in silence. I'll hold a card up and point at someone to come up and put it on the chart. You won't need to raise your hands, because I'm going to have everyone at the back three tables take a turn today." The children listened attentively to my directions.

"Get the last of your wiggles out," I said, "and when I draw the star, we'll all be silent."

This worked perfectly. I suspected it would, as I've used the technique for years. It's especially well suited for an activity such as this one when I want each child to focus. The silence removes interference and allows children to think in their own ways without being interrupted by others' ideas.

I drew the star on the board and had each of the 12 children at the back three tables place a number. All except for Annie placed theirs correctly. She placed 68 in the correct column, but in the 70s row. I pointed to the "8" in 68 and ran my finger up and down the column on the chart,

nodding affirmatively. Then I pointed to the "6" in 68. Annie immediately removed the card and moved it up a row.

After the 12 children had taken their turns, I erased the star. There was a chorus of sighs as they allowed themselves to relax.

I asked the students to talk about the patterns they noticed. Some children had continued to count to locate the spaces for their numbers, but more were seeing and noticing patterns in the array.

Assessing Addition

At this point, I shifted the lesson to find out about the students' ability to combine two-digit numbers. I was interested in gathering information early in the unit about whether students would use the 10s and 1s structure of our number system when faced with an addition problem. The class lesson gave children a way to see addition related to their own experience.

I removed the chart from the wall, turned it around, and replaced it so the children could no longer see the numbers. "We had 39 numbers on the chart after yesterday's class," I said, "and we added 12 more numbers today. How many numbers are on the chart altogether now?" I wrote on the board as I told them the problem:

> 39 yesterday
> 12 more today

"The reason I turned the chart around," I continued, "is that I want to see how you'd solve this problem if you couldn't count the cards. I'm interested in how each of you thinks about this problem, so I want you to work individually. Be sure to explain your reasoning, so I can learn about how you think. Use numbers and words on your paper, and you can draw a picture if it helps you explain how you figured. You may use any materials in the room, but I'm interested in how you would figure this out by yourself, so please don't use a calculator. We'll check later by counting the cards and, if you like, by using a calculator."

The numbers presented a problem of adding with regrouping. If, however, the numbers hadn't required regrouping, I would have restructured it, counting, for example, the number cards in the top five rows and those in the bottom five rows. My goal was to present the children with the challenge of regrouping in a problem-solving situation with which they were familiar.

Note: See page 36 for a rationale and complete description of this assessment and the results from the class.

The Next Few Days

I continued with the 0–99 chart for part of each class over the next several days, using the "Silent Star" method, until the chart was completely filled in. Although I found the "Silent Star" method to be effective, it eliminated letting children convince others why their location was correct. But I was able to see how children approached the problem by watching them at the chart.

NOTE Children often learn from imitating behaviors they observe. By calculating aloud to demonstrate strategies for adding numbers, teachers can model for children ways to think mathematically.

Before beginning each day, I asked the class to figure how many numbers were on the chart already. They counted the cards in each row and I recorded, winding up with a column of ten numbers. I then talked with them about shortcut ways to add the column.

Even though adding a column of ten numbers is beyond the ability of a good part of the class, I took the opportunity to demonstrate different ways to think about numbers. I showed the children how I combined numbers to make 10s, how I looked for doubles to add, and how I added other combinations that I know. I did this all with a light touch, wanting the children to watch me think out loud and perhaps add to their own store of strategies for reasoning numerically.

A Class Discussion

One day, after everyone in the class had a turn placing a number card, only two empty spaces remained on the chart.

"How many numbers are on the chart now?" I asked.

The question sparked several children's thinking, and they presented different ways to think about the problem.

Hassan said, "I know. 100 take away 2 is 98."

Molly said, "You can go 98, then 99, 100."

Andrew said, "If you take 98 and add 2 you get 100, so it has to be 98."

"But it only goes up to 99," Maria said.

"Yeah, there's no 100," Timmy added.

Some of the children still weren't convinced that there were 100 pockets on the chart. This didn't worry me. Earlier in my teaching career, I would have pushed to have all children agree on answers. I've come to realize that I can get all the children to respond correctly that there are 100 numbers on the chart and only 98 on it now, but I can't necessarily get them to believe it or explain why it makes sense. Their understanding comes from their internal processes of constructing. At this time, I noted the children who were having difficulty locating numbers and those who were confused, so I could work with them to find out more about their thinking.

Part 2: Patterns on the 0–99 Chart

About a week after I had taught Part 1 of the lesson, I focused the children on the 0–99 chart in a new way. I told the children I had a game of *Guess My Rule* to play. They were familiar with *Guess My Rule* from the work we had done previously from *Sorting: Groups and Graphs*, one of the books in the *Used Numbers* series. (See Bibliography, page 193.)

"We'll play this game backwards," I said. "I'll tell you the rule and you guess the numbers that fit it. My rule is: All the two-digit numbers on the chart that have both digits the same."

"What does 'digit' mean?" Sarah asked.

"Does anyone know that word?" I asked the class. A few children made attempts, but no one knew the meaning of the word.

"Try guessing numbers for my pattern," I said, "and see if you can figure out what digits are from the guesses." A few children raised their hands. I called on Timmy.

"20," he said.

"No," I answered, "that doesn't fit my rule."

"6," Abby guessed.

"No," I responded, "my number has two digits."

"Oooh, I know," Tomo said, "99."

"Yes," I said, "that's one of my numbers because both of its digits are the same." I removed the card with 99 on it and inserted it so the blank side was showing.

"98," Catherine guessed next.

"No," I responded, "that doesn't fit my rule. Both digits aren't the same."

By now, more than half of the class wanted to give a number. The children were excited. I took a moment to quiet them and called on Molly.

"It's easy," she said. "I guess 22."

"Things are always easy when you know them," I responded, turning the 22 card over to its blank side.

I continued calling on children until I had turned over all the numbers with both digits the same. (In retrospect, I would rather have had some squares of lightly tinted transparency to cover the numbers as they were guessed. Some children were confused when number cards were turned over.)

"Who can explain what 'digit' means?" I asked. Only a few children raised their hands.

"Talk with your partner and see if the two of you can figure out how to explain what digits are," I said. Rather than call on one of the children when only a few seemed to have an idea, I decided to have all of them think about my question.

After a minute or so, I called the class back to attention. "Does anyone have an idea they'd like to report?" I asked. Now about half the children raised their hands. I called on Seth.

"It's like the numbers in a number," he said. "It's just another name."

Katy had something to add. "Some numbers have one digit and some have two."

"Some can have three," Andrew said, "like 245 or something."

"A digit is like a part of a number," Grace said.

I called on a few more children and then changed the direction of the conversation. "Look at the pattern of the blank cards, the ones I turned over because they had both digits the same," I said. "How can you describe the pattern of the blank cards?"

"It goes down on a slant," Molly said.

"It's like stair steps," Teddy said.

"It's a diagonal," Rudy said. We had talked about diagonals of squares in the previous unit, and Rudy had remembered the word.

"It kind of goes from the corner to the other corner," Maria said.

Using Children's Rules

There were no other ideas, and I turned over the cards so that all the numbers were showing again. "Does anyone have a rule that's different from mine?" I asked. Several children raised their hands.

"This time we'll play the game the usual way," I continued. "Don't tell

NOTE Taking time during a lesson to have children talk with their partners is one way for them to explore an idea. It gives students the chance to think before listening to a class discussion. Also, talking in pairs provides the opportunity for more children to verbalize their ideas.

your rule. Call on children to guess numbers, and tell them if their guess fits your rule or not. I'll turn the numbers over for the correct guesses."

I called on Hassan and he came up to the front of the room. I had him whisper his rule to me so I could be a backup check on his responses to the others' guesses. Hassan called on children to guess numbers and I turned the number cards for the correct guesses. When I had turned 10, 30, and 40, some predicted a pattern and figured out Hassan's rule. They soon guessed all the numbers that fit it. Finally, I had Hassan tell his rule. "They're numbers with a zero behind it," he said.

"How would you describe the pattern of Hassan's numbers?" I asked.

"It's just a straight line," Seth said.

"It's all the numbers down one side except for the top one," Leslie said.

"It looks like a flag pole without a flag," Annie said.

"Why do you think that Hassan didn't include zero?" I asked. Hassan looked a bit anxious when I asked this question.

"Because all of his numbers have two numbers," Teddy said.

"You mean two digits," Andrew said, always precise.

"That's it," Hassan said, looking relieved.

"I have a rule to try," Leslie said. Several other children indicated that they also had ideas.

"I'd like to hear all of your ideas," I said. "Here's how. First, I'll give each of you a chance to think of a rule." I showed the children the papers I had prepared with a 0–99 chart reproduced on the top half and lines for writing on the bottom. (See Blackline Masters section, page 180.)

"After you think of a rule that interests you," I said, "color in all the numbers that fit the rule. Then write the rule below the chart and describe the pattern."

"Can we do our rules with the class?" Leslie asked, a bit disappointed that she wasn't getting her turn right then.

"Yes," I said, "I have two ideas about that. Some of you will get to share your rule with the class, and all of you will have your rules in the menu activity." This seemed to satisfy Leslie and the others.

I distributed the sheets and the children got to work. All were engaged and most finished their patterns. Several started a second pattern. Three needed to work on their papers later in the day to complete them.

The Next Day

I began class by playing *Guess My Rule* with some of the rules the children had written. I planned to have several children come to the front of the room and have others guess their rules. Instead of taking the time to have the class guess the numbers, I decided to have children show the numbers that fit their pattern and have others guess the rule and describe the pattern. In this way, I put the emphasis on the verbalization of the rules and description of the patterns, while also preparing the children for the menu task.

"This time, we'll do the activity a little differently," I said. "I'll show you the numbers someone has colored, and you'll guess the rule. Sometimes, people have different ways to describe the same rules, and we'll see if this happens."

The children were eager and interested. I started with Grace's rule. I had Grace come to the front of the room, and I gave her the paper she had done for reference. She had colored in all the numbers with a 6.

Grace colored in all the numbers with a 6 in them.

0–99 Chart

0	1	2	3	4	5	6	7	8	9
10	11	12	13	14	15	16	17	18	19
20	21	22	23	24	25	26	27	28	29
30	31	32	33	34	35	36	37	38	39
40	41	42	43	44	45	46	47	48	49
50	51	52	53	54	55	56	57	58	59
60	61	62	63	64	65	66	67	68	69
70	71	72	73	74	75	76	77	78	79
80	81	82	83	84	85	86	87	88	89
90	91	92	93	94	95	96	97	98	99

My patern is the boxs that have six in it.

I turned the numbers over on the chart and asked the class to guess the rule. Some children seemed confused when the number cards were turned over, so I stopped the lesson and distributed 0–99 charts to each pair of children so they could refer to it. (See page 179.) However, I found that most of the children who were confused didn't find the charts helpful.

I'm not surprised or particularly concerned when children are confused. Rather, it gives me information about how children are thinking at a particular time. At this time, while some of the children were ready and interested in guessing the rule for Grace's pattern, others would benefit from merely guessing the numbers on the cards I had turned over. The class would have a good deal more experience with the 0–99 chart during the unit, however, and I'd have opportunities to watch for changes in individual children's understanding of the structure of numbers on the chart.

I asked for volunteers to guess Grace's rule and called on Sarah.

"The numbers are the 60s," she said.

"That's not it," Grace said. "I colored 16, and that's not in the 60s."

"But you colored in all the 60s," Sarah pointed out.

NOTE Partial understanding and confusion are natural to the learning process. To accommodate differences in children's learning, lessons should allow children to think about mathematical ideas in their own ways and on their own timetables. The goal is to provide students time and opportunities to construct their own understanding.

"It's not my rule," Grace insisted. She called on Nick.

"You did the 60s and the ones that end in 6, too," he said.

Grace looked at me. "That's sort of it, but not how I said it," she said.

"See if anyone has another way to say the rule," I said, "and then you can read the way you wrote it."

Grace called on Amelia. "They have to have a 6 in them," she said.

"That's more like it," Grace said, and she read her rule: *My patern is the boxs that have six in it.*

I thanked Grace and asked her to return to her seat. Then I asked the children to describe what her pattern looked like. I was interested in terminology that would describe the position of the numbers that had been colored. I called on Tomo to give the first description.

"It looks like a pogo stick," he said. Tomo's description seemed to spark a flurry of imaginative remarks that the children found interesting to them. Although the discussion wasn't leading in the direction I had hoped, I recorded all their comments on the board.

"It looks like a cross," Marina said.

"It looks like a lowercase 't,'" Seth offered.

"This is kind of a Halloween idea," Maria said. "It's like the sign on graves in cemeteries."

"That's a cross," Marina said, reiterating her contribution.

"I agree," I said, "but Maria expressed the idea in different words." I recorded Maria's idea. (I take all opportunities to model writing for them.)

As I continued to record their ideas, more and more children raised their hands. When I called on Timmy, he began to get out of his seat to come up to the board and show what he meant. "Just use words, Timmy," I said. "Try and explain your idea."

"See, there are four spaces," he said, "and one is bigger." Timmy was referring to the areas on the 0–99 chart that weren't part of Grace's rule.

Then I listed some other words for them to use to describe the pattern of Grace's numbers: *row, column, top, bottom, middle, horizontal (across), vertical (up and down), diagonal.*

"I find these words helpful for describing patterns on the 0–99 chart," I said. "We used some of them yesterday. Can someone describe Grace's pattern using at least one of these words?" I asked.

Colleen's hand shot up. "I have one, but it's like the others," she said, referring to the ones the other children had offered.

I replied, "Right now, I'd like only descriptions that use at least one of the words I wrote."

I called on Nick. "There's one row and one column," he said.

Next I called on Katy. "One goes across and one goes down, and they're not really in the middle, but kind of."

Only two hands were up now. Clearly, the children were more comfortable with their own words and more interested in their own ideas. I continued, however, pushing to give them more experience with the new words and took two more suggestions.

"There's an up-and-down line and an across line," Gwyn said.

"One goes from top to bottom," Teddy said.

"Let me show you another rule," I said. "This one is Jason's rule." Jason had colored in all the 40s and 50s. Jason came to the front of the room

and I rearranged the number cards on the chart so that all the numbers in the rows of 40s and 50s were turned to their blank sides.
I called on Hassan first.

"All the numbers with 4s and 5s in them," he said. Others nodded. Jason shook his head to indicate that Hassan's guess wasn't correct.

Jason's pattern made a double row on the chart.

0–99 Chart

0	1	2	3	4	5	6	7	8	9
10	11	12	13	14	15	16	17	18	19
20	21	22	23	24	25	26	27	28	29
30	31	32	33	34	35	36	37	38	39
▓	▓	▓	▓	▓	▓	▓	▓	▓	▓
▓	▓	▓	▓	▓	▓	▓	▓	▓	▓
60	61	62	63	64	65	66	67	68	69
70	71	72	73	74	75	76	77	78	79
80	81	82	83	84	85	86	87	88	89
90	91	92	93	94	95	96	97	98	99

All the 40's and 50's

"I notice that Jason didn't color the number 14," I said, "or 15 or 25. Those have a 4 or 5 in them."

"Oh, yeah," Hassan said.

Amelia raised her hand. "I think it's just the 40s and 50s," she said.

Jason confirmed her guess by nodding, looking a little disappointed that he hadn't stumped the class for a longer time. As I had done with Grace's rule, I asked the children to describe the pattern made by the numbers in Jason's rule and I recorded their ideas on the board. Again, their descriptions were imaginative.

"It looks like a row of marching ants all carrying something on their backs," Rudy said.

"It looks like a belt," Jonathan said.

"It's a wide stripe, Grace contributed.

"How about descriptions that use at least one of the words that I recorded?" I requested. I got a few more volunteers this time, but still I wasn't engaging all the children.

"It's a double row," Marina said.

"It goes across in the middle," Gwyn said.

"It's horizontal," Andrew said, "unless you turn it, and then it's vertical."

Next I had Leslie try her rule on the class. She had colored in just four numbers—3, 12, 21, and 30. She had written: *All the ones that equal 3.*

Only four numbers fit Leslie's rule.

0–99 Chart

0	1	2	■	4	5	6	7	8	9
10	11	■	13	14	15	16	17	18	19
20	■	22	23	24	25	26	27	28	29
■	31	32	33	34	35	36	37	38	39
40	41	42	43	44	45	46	47	48	49
50	51	52	53	54	55	56	57	58	59
60	61	62	63	64	65	66	67	68	69
70	71	72	73	74	75	76	77	78	79
80	81	82	83	84	85	86	87	88	89
90	91	92	93	94	95	96	97	98	99

All the ones that equal three.

I had Leslie come to the front of the room, and I turned all the blank cards back to their numbered sides.

"Leslie colored in just four numbers," I said, and the children watched as I turned over the four cards that fit Leslie's rule. The children tried guessing.

"The numbers go 3, 2, 1, 0," Nick said, reading the ones digits down the diagonal. Leslie shook her head to indicate Nick wasn't right.

"It goes 0, 1, 2, 3," Maria said, reading the ones digits from the bottom. Leslie shook her head.

"They're little numbers in the corner," Timmy guessed. Again, Leslie shook her head.

For each guess, I commented that it *could* have been Leslie's rule, but it wasn't the way she wrote it. Leslie was thrilled to be stumping the class. Finally, I asked her to read her rule, and she did so in an unusually strong and confident voice with a big grin. "I did math problems," she said to preface her rule, and then read, "All the ones that equal 3." The children were impressed, but perplexed.

"Explain what you mean by 'equal 3,'" I said.

"Like, 1 plus 2 is 3 and 3 plus 0 is 3," she said.

"How about describing how the pattern looks?" I asked the class.

Marina raised her hand. "It's a teeny diagonal," she said.

"It's a short staircase," Jonathan said.

"It cuts across the corner," Timmy said.

I told the children that they would have other chances to investigate the rest of their patterns. "I'm going to organize your papers for a menu activity," I told them.

ASSESSMENT Numbers on the 0–99 Chart

The problem described below draws on the whole class lesson *The 0–99 Chart*. (See page 22.) Students are asked to add two two-digit numbers with regrouping to figure out how many numbers are on the chart.

For this assessment, do not worry whether the children have been taught the standard procedure for adding with regrouping. The goal here isn't to test children's proficiency with the standard algorithm but rather to test their ability to think and reason mathematically. When children are faced with the problem of combining numbers that require regrouping, and when they haven't been taught the standard procedure for "carrying," they must resort to their own resources. Their search to make sense of the problem and the methods they use to add can provide insights into their understanding of place value and their ability to make use of the 10s and 1s structure of our number system.

Relating the problem to their experience in the whole class lesson provides a context that is familiar to students. In this way, the problem is not an isolated exercise but one that connects to their classroom learning. Also, children should be expected not only to find the numerical answer but also to explain their reasoning. They should be encouraged to explain their thinking with words, numbers, and, if they like, pictures.

Note that when this opportunity for assessment arises as you teach *The 0–99 Chart* lesson to your class, the specific numbers will differ. The goal is to give students a problem that presents them with the need to add with regrouping.

FROM THE CLASSROOM

To introduce the assessment, I removed the 0–99 chart from the wall, turned it around, and replaced it, so the children could no longer see the numbers. "We had 39 numbers on the chart after yesterday's class," I said, "and we added 12 more numbers today. How many numbers are on the chart now?" I wrote on the board as I told them the problem:

> 39 yesterday
> 12 more today

"The reason I turned the chart around," I continued, "is that I want to see how you'd solve this problem if you couldn't count the cards. I'm interested in how each of you thinks about this problem, so I want you to work individually. Be sure to explain your reasoning, so I can learn about how you think. Use numbers and words on your paper, and you can draw if it helps you explain how you figured. Also, you can use any materials in the room, but I'm interested in how you would figure this out by yourself, so please don't use a calculator. We'll check later by counting the cards and, if you like, by using a calculator."

The children's methods for solving this problem fell into five categories. Four children solved the problem by drawing tally marks and counting. Three of those children organized their tallies into fives; Hassan made one long row of lines.

Ten children solved the problem by counting without tally marks. Teddy, for example, wrote: *You tak 39 and ad 12 and you got 51. I cotid in my hed.*

Seth sat next to one of the children who had used tallies. He wrote: *I didet want to do tally marks. I allwase do them so I drew fansey.* He had started with 40 and written 12 numbers, which brought him to 51.

Seth solved the problem by counting on from 39.

Three children displayed their understanding of place value in their solutions. As is typical for children who invent their own algorithms, all of these children started their calculations with the 10s. Rudy, for example, wrote: *I solved by doing math first I did 3 + 1 is 4 but then I did 9 + 2 so I had a extra 10 so I came up with 51.* He had written the problem vertically.

Rudy's solution showed his understanding of place value.

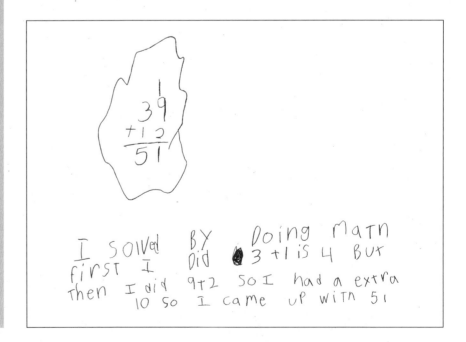

Leslie wrote the problem horizontally and explained: *I had 4 tens and then I added 11 and I cared 1 and I cam up with 51. I think the answer is 51.*

Andrew wrote *39 + 12* horizontally and then wrote *40 + 11* vertically underneath. He wrote: *1. Add the tens you get 40 2. Add the ones you get 11.*

Three other children used the standard algorithm and each got the correct answer. However, none of the three could explain the sense of the method they used.

Tomo, for example, wrote: *I did it at a nuder* [another] *scool near japantown.* When I asked him to explain why his solution made sense, he said, "That's how I learned it."

Grace wrote: *I did 39 + 12. 9 + 2 = 11 so I had to carie the one up to the ather number so three + one = 4 so I had to add one more because I caried one up and that makes 5 so it is 51.* I asked Grace why her method for adding made sense. "My mother taught me," she said.

I circled the "1" she had carried and wrote on her paper: *What does the "little 1" mean?*

She wrote back: *I don't know.*

Grace could use the standard algorithm, but when asked to explain the meaning of the "little 1," she didn't know.

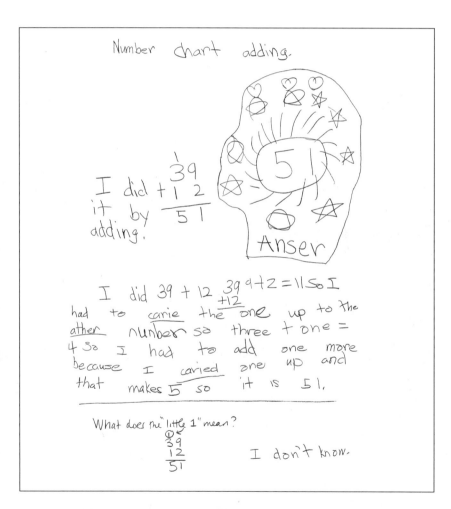

Marina had also gotten the answer of 51, seemingly by using the standard algorithm, but her written explanation didn't make sense. She wrote:

I added 3 + 1 and put down five and I thot I was right. I cowntid my fingers. I added 9 and then I added 2. So I added it up and put down a 5 and 1 and I got 51. "I learned to do it this way last year in first grade," she told me.

Marina's paper shows her consistent use of an incorrect algorithm.

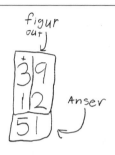

To chek   I added 3+1 and put down five and I
thot I was right. I
cowntid my I added 9 and then I added 2. So I added
fingers.   it up and put down a 5 and 1 and I got 51.

$$\begin{array}{r} 2\!\!\!/6 \\ +1\!\!\!/7 \\ \hline 31 \end{array}$$

I did 2 plus
1 is 3 and 6+7 is 13 so
I put the 1 on the paper
and it is 31. the
3 dosint mater because
you all ways put the number
first.

I turned her paper over and asked if she would do another problem so I could watch her. She agreed. I wrote:

$$\begin{array}{r} 26 \\ +17 \\ \hline \end{array}$$

Marina quickly wrote down a "3" in the tens column and, after thinking a few moments, wrote a "1" in the ones column. I asked her to write an explanation of her method. Her description was similar to how she did the other problem. She wrote: *I did 2 plus 1 is 3 and 6 + 7 is 13 so I put the 1*

NOTE Answers alone are not sufficient or accurate indicators of children's mathematical power. Having children explain their reasoning processes is important in all instances, whether their responses are correct or incorrect. Only when students explain their thinking can teachers gain insights into what they do and don't understand.

Sarah counted on her fingers but came up with the wrong answer.

on the paper and it is 31. She brought her paper to me and read what she had written.

"How did you know to put the 1 from the 13 in the answer?" I asked her. "Can you write about that?"

Marina nodded. She returned to her seat and wrote: *the 3 dosint mater because you allways put the number first.* When she read it to me, she told me she meant that you always were supposed to use the first number and that's why she put down the 1 and didn't use the 3.

"Can you explain that?" I probed.

"That's how I learned it," she said with confidence. "It's the rule."

I showed her the solution she got for 39 plus 12. "Oops," she said, "3 plus 1 is 4. It should be 41."

I then realized that her correct answer to the first problem was just luck. Over and over, I get evidence that children's correct answers can hide confusion, and I'm reminded of the importance of probing children's thinking and having them explain their reasoning.

The other three children's papers revealed their lack of ability to deal with the problem at all. They wrote some numbers on their papers, and two of them wrote down answers they had gotten from others, but none could explain their work.

Sarah wrote: *I counted on my fingers.*

This range of abilities and methods isn't unusual. My goal, of course, is for every child to understand how the 10s and 1s structure of our number system can help them make sense of numerical calculations. But I know that children learn on their own timetables. My goal is a long-range one, and I collect information to judge how children's ideas are changing and to look for clues about how I might help each one understand mathematics more fully.

WHOLE CLASS LESSON   Stars in One Minute

Overview

Children need many experiences counting large numbers of objects and connecting their counting to our number system. *Stars in One Minute* provides children experience with thinking about ways to organize and count a large quantity of objects. The students draw stars for one minute and count them in several ways. Extra bonuses of the lesson are that children get experience timing one minute and organizing their results into a class graph and interpreting the data.

Note: The first two parts of this lesson, taught to a different class of children than described in this unit, appears on Part 1 of the videotape series *Mathematics: Teaching for Understanding*. (For information, see the Bibliography, page 193.)

Before the lesson

Gather these materials:
■ If there isn't a class clock with a sweep second hand, collect about half a dozen time keepers
■ 3-by-3-inch Post-it™ Notes, one per child

Teaching directions

This lesson has three parts, each requiring one math period. In my class one year, I actually spread Part 3 of the lesson over four days, as I describe in the *From the Classroom* section. In part, this was due to my choice to have the class repeat part of the lesson to collect data for the class graph. In part, it was because I chose to allow time for the children to reflect on what we did before pushing further. Another year, I did the lesson in three days as I've explained below, and it worked fine.

No matter how well I plan a lesson, I can never plan students' responses. The more thinking I do about my teaching and the more experience I have with a lesson, the better able I am to make changes as situations change. For this reason, I've included both variations on this lesson to offer options for thinking about it in more than one way.

Note that the math periods for this lesson do not have to be consecutive. Sometimes, when children have time away from an activity, they're better able to reflect on what they've already done. Also, once you've introduced a few of the menu activities, and children complete work from a whole class lesson at different rates, they can choose activities from the menu.

Part 1: Introducing the Activity

■ Begin the lesson by asking the children what they know about one minute. If you have a class clock with a sweep second hand, talk about how it measures one minute. Otherwise, you'll have to rely on your watch or bring to class some time keepers for the children to use.

■ After all of the students have had a chance to tell their ideas about one minute, ask them to put their heads down and try and guess how long a minute is. Tell them that you'll say "Start" when you begin timing and

"Stop" when one minute has passed. They should lift their heads when they think a minute has gone by. If they lift their heads before you've said stop, they should wait quietly.

■ Ask the children to predict how many stars they think you could draw on the board in one minute. Record their predictions on the board.

■ Have the students time one minute while you draw stars.

■ After you've drawn stars for one minute, ask the children to suggest ways to count the stars. Tell them you want to count them several different ways to be sure you've counted correctly. Because this lesson prepares the children for counting objects in the menu activities, choose from their suggestions ways that involve grouping the objects into different size groups, including 2s, 5s, and 10s. If none of the children suggests grouping, make the suggestion yourself.

■ Count the stars several different ways, involving the children in helping you do so.

■ Optional: If you'd like to incorporate a children's book into the lesson, this is a good time to read the book *Draw Me a Star* by Eric Carle. (See the Children's Books section, page 168.) The book has bold illustrations and a simple story line about a young artist who draws a five-pointed star and then continues through his life to draw the sun, a tree, flowers, clouds, the moon, night, and, finally, as an old man, an eight-pointed star. At the end of the book, Carle presents a step-by-step procedure for drawing an eight-pointed star.

Part 2: The Children Draw Stars

■ In another math period, discuss with the class the different kinds of stars they know how to draw. Draw a few on the board—a five-pointed star, an asterisk, a six-pointed star, an eight-pointed star. Have volunteers come to the board and show other kinds of stars that they know how to draw.

■ Tell the children that you'll time one minute while they draw stars. Before starting the minute, give students some time to choose one kind of star and practice drawing it on scratch paper.

■ Time one minute while the children make their stars. Have them count their stars in at least two ways and write about the methods they used. It's helpful to put a prompt on the board:

> I counted by ___.
> I counted by ___.
> I drew ___ stars.

■ When children finish their work, check to see that they've counted their stars in at least two ways and got the correct answer both times. If not, have them recheck and revise their work.

■ Each time a child brings you a correct paper, ask: *If you circled 10s, how many circles would you have to make?* It's likely that not many, if any, chose to group their stars by 10s. However, asking this question can help you assess their understanding.

Part 3: Making a Class Graph

■ As in Part 2, have the children once again draw stars for one minute and count the stars in two ways. Distribute 3-by-3-inch Post-its to the children, and have them draw a sample star, write their names, and record the number of stars they got. Ask them to put their Post-its on the chalkboard.

■ Talk with the class about how they might organize the Post-its into a graph so they can see the different kinds of stars they drew. (One nice thing about Post-its is that you can move them easily to try out several suggestions.) Finally, select one way and put the Post-its on chart paper.

■ Ask the children to think about the information on the graph of Post-its. Have children explain what the graph shows while you record their ideas on a chart. If you want, ask children to figure out the number of stars drawn in each category or by the children in the class altogether. These problems provide a sensible reason for children to use calculators.

■ Leave the graph posted on the wall for up to a week, giving children a chance to see and think about it. Then ask the children to look at the graph and think about sentences that would describe what they noticed. Call on children to give their ideas.

■ Post large chart paper and explain that you'd like to write about a dozen sentences about the graph. Ask students for sentences that describe the data on the graph. Record the sentences on the chart paper.

■ Give students the homework assignment for *Stars in One Minute.* (See the Homework section, page 172.)

FROM THE CLASSROOM

Part 1: Introducing the Lesson

I began the *Stars in One Minute* activity by asking the children what they knew about one minute.

"It takes 60 minutes to make an hour," Nick said.

"There are 60 seconds in a minute," Gwyn offered.

"We have 10 minutes for recess," Jason said.

"The big hand on the clock is the minute hand," Katy said.

"The fast hand goes all the way around in one minute," Leslie said. Some of the children didn't know what she meant and since our class clock doesn't have a sweep second hand, I couldn't explain without showing them my watch. I decided it would be too disruptive to show my watch, as all the children would want to see it, so I continued calling on other children who were interested in contributing their ideas.

"My watch blinks every second," Timmy added. He was proud of the digital watch he had received for his birthday.

"Mine can be a stop watch," Rudy said, "but I can't remember how to work it."

After all the children who wanted had told their ideas, I gave the next direction. "We're going to do an experiment that will give you an idea of how long a minute is," I said. "In a moment, I'll ask you to put your heads down. I'll say 'Start' and you'll keep your heads down until you think one minute has passed. I'll watch my watch and say 'Stop' when a minute is up. If you lift your head before I say 'Stop,' just wait quietly while I finish timing."

"Can I look at my watch and time too?" Nick asked. Several others with watches wanted to know if this was OK.

"You can either time along with me and see if we get to one minute at the same time," I said, "or put your head down and try to guess when a minute is up."

"Is it OK to count to 60?" Sarah asked.

"Yes," I said, "you can do whatever you'd like to try and guess how long a minute takes."

"Why should I count to 60?" Maria asked.

"Because there are 60 seconds in a minute," Sarah said, "and you go 1, one thousand, 2, one thousand, 3, one thousand, like that."

"I don't get it," Maria said.

"I don't either," Colleen said.

Not all the children in the class could tell time or knew about seconds and minutes. I gave enough information so all could participate in the experiment. "You don't have to count as Sarah suggested," I said. "She thinks it will be helpful because she's learned that there are 60 seconds in one minute, and she has a way of counting that she thinks can help keep track of seconds."

"But what do we do?" Maria asked.

"Try and guess how long one minute is," I said. "I'll say 'Start' and 'Stop,' and you have to try and feel how long a minute takes."

I got the children settled with their heads down, said "Start," and began to time. When a minute had passed, I said "Stop."

"We came out the same time," Nick said. He had decided to time on his watch.

"So that's how long one minute is," I said. "Now I want you to make a prediction about how many stars you think I could draw on the board in one minute."

"What kind of stars?" Tomo asked.

"Like this," I said, drawing a five-pointed star on the board.

Most of the children were interested in predicting. I wrote their guesses on the board, putting tally marks after each to show the number of children who made the same estimate. Their guesses ranged from 15 to 200.

It was too bad that I hadn't thought to bring a clock from home with a sweep second hand so the children could have timed me. Instead, I asked Caroline, the student teacher, to time one minute while I drew stars. "If you have a watch," I said, "you can keep time as well."

Counting the Stars

After one minute, I had filled the board with stars and asked the children for ways to count them. They had lots of suggestions.

"Erase them one-by-one," Katy said, "and draw them on the other side of the board, and the class can count as you do it."

"Just draw a circle around each star as you count it," Leslie said.

"Count by 2s and draw circles around them," Rudy said.

"Even though they're not in good rows, they're kind of in rows," Andrew said, "so you can count the rows and then add up the numbers like we did with the 0–99 chart."

"Circle 5s and count," Marina said.

"Color in each star and count," Grace said.

"I have another idea," Andrew said. "Count by 20s and circle them. You won't have to draw so many circles or add so many numbers that way."

"We don't have time to try all of your methods," I said. "Let me try some that I think you'll be able to use when you count your own stars. First I'll count by 2s." I circled groups of two and had the children count by 2s as I did so. They got stuck a few times, going from 18 to 20, and then again from 28 to 30. Changing from one decade to the other is often hard for children. We counted 59 stars.

"If you get stuck counting by 2s," I said, "you can always use the 0–99 chart to help." I had them practice counting by 2s, following my finger as I pointed to the numbers on the chart.

"Did anyone notice a pattern of the numbers I pointed to?" I asked.

"You skipped every other one," Marina said.

No one else volunteered an idea, so I continued by suggesting a different way to count.

"If I count the stars again, this time by 5s," I said, "would I get 59 again?"

"You can't count by 5s," Teddy said. "It wouldn't come out right."

"What do you mean?" I asked.

"You would have some outside the circles," he answered.

"You mean like having this extra star outside the circle when I grouped by 2s?" I asked. He nodded.

"That doesn't bother me," I said. "I can count the extras at the end. Watch and you'll see how. But will I still get 59 stars?"

"You have to," Hassan said, "you have the same stars."

"Yeah," Andrew said, "it's the same."

"Well, it could be different," Colleen said. From my past experience doing this lesson with other classes, I've found that while it's obvious to some children that the number of stars will be the same no matter how I count them, others aren't sure.

I then circled groups of five, using another color, and the children counted. When we reached 55, I counted the extras, "56, 57, 58, 59."

"I'm going to count one more way," I said, "to be sure that I've drawn 59 stars. I'm going to count by 10s. How many circles will I have to draw if I circle 10s?"

A few children raised their hands—Andrew, Rudy, Leslie, Marina, Jonathan, and Hassan. Others didn't seem to have a clue. Although all the children could count by 10s, this didn't mean they understood the

NOTE Teaching by telling doesn't help children construct their own understanding. Making sense of place value requires that children connect, for themselves, the meaning of the digits in numbers to the structure of our place value system. They need many experiences counting large quantities of objects and relating the quantities to their numerical representations.

relationship of grouping by 10s to written numerals or numerical quantities. The children counted along with me. Each time we reached 10, I stopped and circled 10 stars, and then began counting again with 1. After circling five groups of ten and seeing that there were nine extras, I invited the children to count the stars with me. Most joined in after I got started, "10, 20, 30, 40, 50, 51, 52, 53, 54, 55, 56, 57, 58, 59."

"I knew when I wrote 59, right after I counted by 2s, that there would be five 10s," I said. "It's easy for me because the first number tells how many 10s there are and the other tells the extras." I offered this information to see if any of the children commented or indicated confirmation by nodding or in some other way. I did not offer the information with the goal of having children learn about 10s and 1s. Rather, I offered the information with a light touch, conversationally, with no implied "this is important" tone or purpose, to make it available should any child find it useful. I planned to point out how 10s and 1s relate to numbers over and over during the unit and throughout the year.

Drawing Stars

About 20 minutes still remained, and I gathered the children on the rug to read *Draw Me a Star* by Eric Carle. The children liked the book. The illustrations were bold and the story invited them to predict what the author would draw next. Also, the book provided directions for making one type of eight-pointed star, which intrigued a good number of the children.

I had the children return to their seats. I drew four different stars on the board—a five-pointed star, a six-pointed star, an asterisk, and an eight-pointed star—and labeled them. I spent a little time showing the children how to draw an eight-pointed star.

I asked for volunteers to draw different kinds of stars. Teddy drew a five-pointed star by just drawing the outline. Eli drew a four-pointed star. Colleen did a different kind of eight-pointed star. Marina and Julie drew stars that were essentially the same as the one Teddy drew, but they looked different enough for the children to agree they were different.

I gave the children 6-by-9-inch pieces of newsprint on which they could practice making stars. They made a great variety of stars, and several were interested in figuring out how to make the eight-pointed star in the book.

Seth noticed that the five-pointed star took five lines and the eight-pointed star took eight lines. His discovery sparked others to investigate the number of lines it took for stars with other numbers of points. Their conclusion was that the number of points and lines *could* match, but did not have to. "It depends on the kind of star you make," Leslie said.

It was an active lesson and the children were fully engaged.

Part 2: The Children Draw Stars

I told the children that today I would time one minute while they drew stars. "First, think about the kind of star you're going to draw," I said.

"Do we have to draw just one kind of star?" Seth asked.

"Yes," I said, "I'd like you to choose one kind of star to draw. That way, we can do the experiment again another time, and you can see which kind of star is quicker for you to draw."

"Can't we do two stars?" Annie asked.

"I want you to choose just one kind," I said, repeating my directions.

"This isn't a contest to see who draws the most stars," I added. "It's not a race. It's an experiment, and we'll see what we can learn."

While timing one minute, I noticed that Timmy wasn't able to draw a star. Several times, he started a star and erased it, and he was getting frustrated and upset. I whispered to him that I'd teach him in just a little while and asked him to wait at the back table for me.

After one minute, I asked the children to count their stars in at least two different ways. I gave them each another sheet of paper and said, "Record the number of stars you drew and write about how you counted them. Remember, you've got to count in at least two different ways."

Leslie grouped by 2s and 4s and drew 8 stars.

NOTE Confusion for students typically exists when a new activity asks them to do something with which they're not familiar. However, the confusion typically settles down once they feel more secure with what they are to do. It's important not to make instructional decisions just to avoid confusion but to remember the potential benefit to children of facing new challenges and having new experiences.

Some of the children were uncertain and uncomfortable with the task. I rushed about, helping children get settled and started. Mostly, I'd ask children to tell me one way to count the stars. Typically, they'd answer "by 1s," "by 2s," or "by 5s." "That's a good way," I'd respond, "and be sure to show on your stars paper how you did it and then explain on the other sheet.

Finally, I remembered Timmy waiting for me at the back table. He was sitting patiently. I brought him a clean sheet of paper, had him hold a pencil, and guided his hand to show him how to draw a five-pointed star. I did this four times, each time saying, "Up, down, left, right, connect." I thought that the combination of the movement with the words would help. He then tried one by himself but started down instead of up. I took his

hand again and did three more. Then he did one right, followed by two more. "Keep practicing," I said, "and I'll be back in a minute."

I returned to supervising the rest of the class. Most were settled into their work. Two were finished, or thought they were, and brought their papers to me. I accepted Marina's, stapling her star paper to her written description. She had written: *I counted by twos. I count by ones.* She had recorded 24 on her stars paper.

"Can I do the menu now?" she asked.

"No," I replied. "There are only ten minutes left, and I haven't taught you the activities for the new menu. Take this time to read quietly."

Rudy drew 42 five-pointed stars.

I counted by 5s.
I counted by 2s.
I drew 42 stars

I then read Nick's paper, but I didn't accept it. It said: *I counted by 2s.* He had circled the stars in groups of two.

"You didn't record how many stars you drew," I said. "And you've only counted one way. You've got to count at least two ways so you have a check on your work." Nick groaned and returned to his seat.

I went to the back of the room. Timmy now had a sheet full of stars. "Would you like me to time one minute while you draw stars?" I asked. He nodded yes. I gave him a fresh sheet of paper and started timing, watching the time as I read more children's work.

After reading several more papers, I realized how difficult this was for the children. It was the third week of October, and the children were still adjusting to new routines. They weren't yet comfortable with writing, and writing in math class was still new for them. With this task, I didn't insist

on much revision. I decided to accept their work and try the activity again another time.

By the end of class, I had papers from almost all of the children. Four or five children were still working on theirs. About ten children were on the rug, reading silently. Others were at their desks reading.

Gwyn drew 24 asterisks and noticed there were 4 extras when she grouped by 5s.

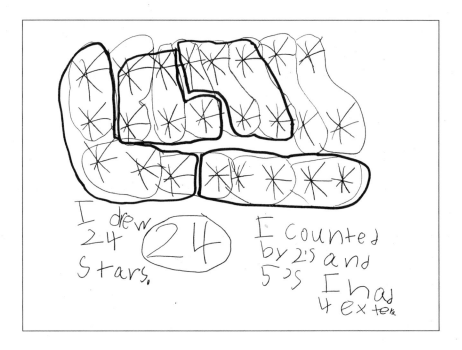

I drew 24 Stars. 24 I counted by 2's and 5's I had 4 exten

Part 3: Making a Class Graph

A few days later, I again had the children draw stars and write about their methods. Because they were already familiar with the activity, I felt they would be better able to describe their methods in writing, and I wanted to use this opportunity to help them become more comfortable with writing in math class. Also, I wanted to collect their data for a class graph.

I began class by telling the children that they were going to draw stars again. "Just as we did last time," I said, "I'll time one minute while you draw stars." The children were eager to do the activity again.

"There's something a little different I want to do this time," I said. I showed them a pad of 3-by-3-inch Post-its. Several of them were familiar with Post-its and wanted to describe how their parents used them.

"After you draw and count your stars," I continued, "and show me your paper about the two ways you counted them, I'll give you one of these Post-its. On it, you are to write your name, draw a sample star to show which kind you did, record the number you got, and post it on the board."

For a few minutes, I let the children practice drawing the kind of stars they were planning to use for the activity. Then I called them to attention and began timing. After the minute was up, I reminded the children to count the stars they drew in two different ways. "That's so you'll have a check on your counting," I said.

This time, the children were much more willing and able to write about their counting methods. The lesson went very smoothly. By having students

NOTE Lessons often are more successful the second time. When children are familiar with what's expected of them, they're more comfortable, can focus better on the assignment, and engage more fully with the mathematics.

show me their papers before getting Post-its, I was able to check their work. If they didn't show how they counted in at least two ways, or if they didn't record the number of stars they drew, I had them revise their papers.

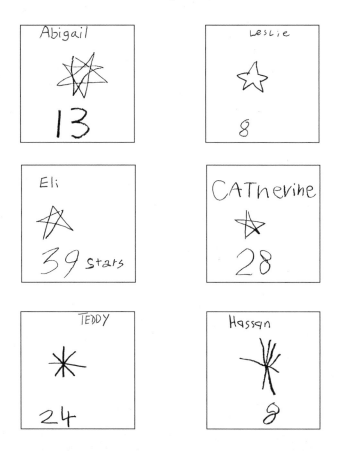

The most frequent method they used was to count by grouping their stars into 2s. (Of the 24 children present, 18 used grouping by 2s as one of their methods.) Counting by 5s and 1s was also popular. None of the children chose to group by 10s. This didn't surprise me, as my experience has been the same whenever I've taught this lesson. However, as each child brought me a paper to get a Post-it, I asked, "If you circled 10s, how many circles would you have to make?" All but six children were able to answer correctly.

When all the children had completed the assignment, the Post-its were randomly arranged on the board. I counted 26 children in the class. "Let's check to make sure everyone's Post-it is here," I said.

I counted the Post-its three ways—by 2s, 5s, and 10s. Each time, I drew circles around the Post-it groups and had the students count. Before grouping by 10s, I asked the class, "How many circles do you think I'll have to make?" About two-thirds of the children raised their hands.

I then asked the class for suggestions to organize the Post-its. Sarah came up with the idea of sorting them by the kinds of stars. I did this, arranging the Post-its into a bar graph with five categories. There were 5 asterisks, 13 five-pointed stars, 4 eight-pointed stars, 1 cross, and 1 different-looking five-pointed star, with only the outline drawn.

NOTE Although grouping by 10s is an essential part of the numerical symbolism for our place value system, it seems unwieldy for children to make groups of 10 when counting large collections of objects. They more naturally group by 2s or 5s, or count by 1s. I think it's important not to impose counting by 10s on students but to take every opportunity to connect the 10s and 1s structure to the children's counting experiences and to written numerals.

We talked about the different number of stars in each row. Children were quick to report that there was one more asterisk than eight-pointed stars, and four more asterisks than crosses. But comparing the row of five-pointed stars (13) and asterisks (5) was difficult for most of them. Figuring "how many more" is difficult for students of this age. The children offered a few different methods for figuring.

Jason said, "I know that 8 plus 5 is 13, so it has to be 8."

Grace thought about it differently. "I know that 10 plus 3 is 13 and that 10 take away 5 is 5," she said, "so I did 5 plus 3 and got 8."

Teddy was more concrete in his approach. "I just saw where they lined up," he said, "and counted the extras." He came up to show the Post-its he had counted.

Katy then noticed the numbers on the Post-its. "They're all different," she said, "and they're out of order."

I put the five Post-its in the asterisks row in numerical order. "That's going to be more difficult with the five-pointed stars," I said, "because there are more to rearrange."

"Can I do it?" Hassan asked. I agreed, and he came up to the front of the room. It was complicated to move all the Post-its, but with help from the rest of the class, Hassan finally accomplished the task.

Stars in One Minute

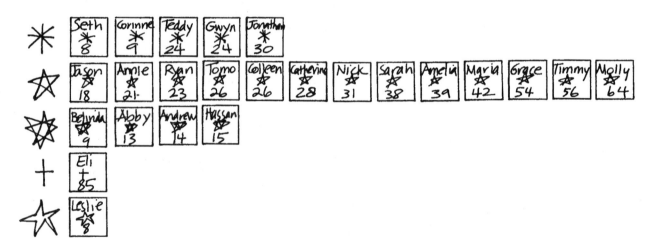

The children enjoyed the activity. It especially appealed to Rudy's need for order. "When the Post-its were all over the board," he said, "it didn't look like anything. But now it's good."

The graph showed the different kinds of stars the children had drawn, with the Post-its in each category ordered by numbers of stars. After class, I transferred the Post-its to a piece of chart paper so we could talk about the graph at a later time.

Revisiting the Graph

I waited a week before processing the *Stars in One Minute* graph. I did this for several reasons. One was to continue introducing other activities in

the unit. Children enjoy having a variety of activities and a change of pace. Also, I've found that when a graph is posted for a while, children have the chance, if they're interested, to think about the data. Even if children don't focus on it, they become familiar with it and come to discussions fresh and interested.

Near the end of class one day, when about 20 minutes remained, I asked the children to look at the graph and think about sentences that would describe what they noticed. I had several of them give their ideas orally. Then I posted three 12-by-18-inch sheets of white paper and told the children that I'd like to write a dozen sentences about the graph.

"How many make a dozen?" I asked. About half the class raised their hands and I called on Jonathan. He knew it was 12.

"I plan to write four sentences on each sheet of paper," I said. "Let's see if that will get us to 12. How much is 4 plus 4?" That was easy for most of the children.

"And how much is 8 plus 4 more?" I continued. That was easy for fewer of them. I try to integrate numerical problems such as this one into lessons whenever possible. Not only does it give children a chance to think about numbers, it brings numerical reasoning into situations on a regular basis.

"If I write four sentences on each paper," I said, "which number sentence will be at the top of the third sheet?" The class seemed interested in this question, and I waited until almost two-thirds of them had raised their hands. I could see that several were counting to themselves, pointing at the sheets as they did so.

I called on Grace and she answered, "Nine." I wrote a 9 at the top of the third sheet.

"As we write our sentences," I said, "we'll be able to check if that's the right place for 9." (I wonder what I would have done if Grace had answered incorrectly. I think I'd have asked her how she figured. And this reminds me that I accepted her answer without having her explain her reasoning. I didn't ask Jonathan to explain his answer to the number in a dozen because it is, I think, purely social knowledge. But Grace had to do some reasoning to come up with her response. It's hard to remember to ask all the time. We need to remind ourselves to do so.)

I wrote the sentences as the children offered them, recording the language they used:

1. Most children did a 5-pointed star.

2. The most 5-pointed stars was Nick's with 64.

3. The two stars with the least Post-its were the cross and the outline of the 5-pointed star.

4. There are two kinds of 5-pointed stars.

5. The student who made the most stars in the whole entire class was Eli with 85 stars.

6. The 8-pointed row is the only row with three numbers in order. (There were four Post-its in the row with the numbers 9, 13, 14, and 15 on them.)

7. There are 24 Post-its altogether.

When Sarah made the observation that there were 24 Post-its, I stopped and focused the class on the calculation. "Let's check," I said, and wrote down the number of Post-its in each row as I counted them:

5
13
4
1
1

Several children volunteered to solve the problem and came to the board to do so. Amelia did it by adding 13 and 5 to get 18, then adding 18 and 4 to get 22, and finally adding 22 and 2 to get 24. In a sense, she was counting on.

Teddy explained a different method. "I did 4 plus 1 is 5," he said, "and another 5 makes 10. And I added that to the 10 to get 20." He was talking about the "1" in 13. "And then there is 4 more, so it's 24."

Leslie had another way. "You go 10 plus 5 is 15," she began, taking 10 from the 13 and the 5. "Then 4 and 1 is 5 so 15 plus 5 is 20. And then you have a 3 and a 1 left, and that makes 4, so it's 20 plus 4 and that's 24."

Timmy raised his hand. "I know because I counted," he said.

I then asked for another sentence to add to the chart. Tomo raised his hand. "There are 95 asterisks," he said, stumbling over the word "asterisks" and asking for help in pronouncing it. Tomo had been adding all the numbers in the asterisks row while the others were working on the total number of Post-its.

"How did you figure that out?" I asked, listing the numbers from the five Post-its in the asterisks row:

8
19
24
24
30

As I wrote the numbers, I rounded off and estimated the sum to myself, adding 10, 20, 20, 20, and 30 to get 100. "I think that 95 is close," I said, "but I think it isn't large enough."

The children shifted their attention to this problem. Several reached for pencil and paper. I started to figure out loud and record to model for the class one way to do the adding. I added the 10s first and got 80. Then I added the ones, combining 8 and 9 to get 17 and the two 4s to get 8 and then adding 17 and 8 to get 25. By the time I started to add 80 and 25, Tomo changed his mind.

"It's 105," he said. "I fixed it."

I contined with my work to verify his solution. Several others agreed. Only about seven children were involved with this calculation. For most, the numbers were too large, so I didn't dwell on it. I recorded Tomo's corrected sentence on the board.

8. There are 105 asterisks.

"Can I figure out how many stars there are altogether?" Andrew asked. This is just the kind of challenge that Andrew loves.

"We already did it," Jason called out. "It's 24."

"No," Andrew said, "I'm going to figure out all the stars on all the Post-its." Jason was still confused, but some of the others caught on and also wanted to start working on the problem. Eli and Sean got up to get paper. I asked them to sit down and give me their attention.

"I'll write Andrew's suggestion," I said, "and put a blank for the number until we figure it out." I recorded on the list:

9. There are _____ stars on all the Post-its.

"We'll see what Andrew comes up with and then the rest of you can also try if you'd like," I said. "And we'll add more sentences to our chart tomorrow." I felt that the discussion had gone long enough and wanted to change the pace. Also, I've learned that when I stretch an investigation over several days, children have time to think about it, and their participation often increases. I had the children start work on menu activities.

The Next Day

At the beginning of class, Andrew asked to make a report. "There are 715 stars altogether," he announced. I decided to have all who were interested check Andrew's answer with a calculator. Most had used calculators before, and they were available to the children at any time. But not many had shown much interest. This situation gave me a chance to encourage them to use calculators for a problem that they wanted to solve and could not really do any other way.

On the board, I recorded the numbers from each of the Post-its so there were five columns.

✳	✶	✷	✛	☆
8	18	9	85	8
19	21	13		
24	23	14		
24	26	15		
30	26	—		
—	28	51		
105	31			
	38			
	39			
	42			
	54			
	56			
	64			
	—			
	466			

As children reported sums, I wrote them for each column so that the others could check. Some diligently worked on the problem, others made up problems of their own or just explored with the calculator, and others chose a task from the menu. Some of the children using the calculators were fascinated by the "M" that appeared in the display and were experimenting with making it come and go; others didn't notice it or weren't interested. There are such differences among children!

One More Day

The next day, I continued having the children report sentences to add to our list. I had left the columns of numbers on the board, and it inspired the next sentence.

10. There are 51 8-pointed stars.

11. There are two 24s in the asterisk row.

12. There are two 26s in the 5-pointed row.

"Can I give one more?" Gwyn asked. I agreed and squeezed her idea on the last sheet.

13. There are 13 5-pointed stars and 11 of all the others.

I used Gwyn's sentence to pose a problem. "Would you say that more than or less than half of the stars on our graph are five-pointed stars?" I asked. After a few moments, three children had raised their hands. Most were perplexed by the problem.

"This question may be too hard for second graders," I said. "But if you'd like to work on it, then do so. If not, choose an activity from the menu." The children got to work.

WHOLE CLASS LESSON   Counting Fish

Overview

In *Counting Fish,* children group and count objects in several ways. The lesson uses 3/4-inch interlocking cubes to help children connect the 10s and 1s structure of our number system to a concrete material. The lesson is similar in intent to *Stars in One Minute,* but the new context and the use of the cubes make it different enough to be fresh and interesting for the students. Also, interlocking cubes can be easily organized into different-size groups and counted in several ways. Although the description provides details for a specific lesson, the overall structure of the lesson can be applied to other contexts. Suggested variations on this lesson offer additional ways children can count.

Before the lesson

Gather these materials:
■ Interlocking cubes, either Multilink, Snap, or Unifix cubes, two per child
■ A bucket, bowl, or other container large enough to hold the cubes

Teaching directions

■ Have each child put two cubes into the bucket. (I used a plastic fish bowl and, on a suggestion from one of the children, my students decided to call the cubes "fish." This is not an essential part of the lesson, as the lesson worked just as well when I called it *Cubes in a Bucket.* But the imaginary context captured my students' interest and I've used it in other situations even when I didn't have a container that looked like a fish bowl.)

■ Write on the board the number of students in class. Then ask the children to figure out the number of cubes in the bucket and explain their reasoning. Put a prompt on the board to help them start their writing:

There are ____ fish in the bowl. I think this because
_____.

■ After all the children have completed their papers (and perhaps the next day), gather the class for a discussion. Have several students show their papers and share their solutions. Discuss the variety of methods and recording systems they used.

■ Remove the cubes from the bucket, snapping them into trains of two cubes each, and stand the trains in a row so the class can see them and count with you. You may want to review first with the children how to count by 2s.

■ Ask the children to predict how many trains there would be if you rearranged the cubes into trains with five in each. Ask if they think there would be extra cubes. Rearrange the cubes and count the number of trains and extras. Then count by 5s to verify the number of cubes. (Not all children may be convinced that the total number of cubes stays the same when they're rearranged!)

■ Ask students to predict how many trains and extra cubes there would be if you rearranged the cubes into trains of 10. Give all children who have ideas the chance to express them. Then rearrange the cubes into trains of 10, count the number of trains and extras, and finally count the cubes by 10s to verify the total.

■ From time to time, engage the children in other counting experiences, varying the contexts and materials. Each time, have the children put the objects into groups of 2 or 5 and then count. Ask children to predict how many groups of 10 and extras there would be. Verify with the materials. Try the following:

1. Repeat *Counting Fish,* having students each put three, four, or five cubes into the bucket.

2. Have the children put one cube in each of their pockets and then make a train to show how many they have. Ask them to predict the number of pockets in the entire class, then organize the cubes into trains with two in each and count to find the total. Have them predict the number of groups of five and ten cubes they can make and explain their reasoning. Verify with the cubes. Repeat for several days and compare the different numbers of pockets. (A complete description of this lesson is in Chapter 6 of *A Collection of Math Lessons From Grades 1 Through 3;* see the Bibliography, page 193.)

3. Ask the children to bring pennies from home for a class penny jar and count how many there are, again by 2s, 5s, and 10s. Continue over several days and then have the class decide what they can buy with their money. You may want to read *A Chair for My Mother* by Vera B. Williams to stimulate interest in collecting pennies. (For additional information, see the Bibliography, page 193.)

4. Count the number of buttons in the class. Have each child take one bean or cube for each button on his or her clothing. Count in several ways as you did for the fish and pockets. Repeat for several days and compare the counts.

FROM THE CLASSROOM

I brought out a plastic bowl and asked each child to put in two Snap Cubes. "Who remembers how many children are here today?" I asked.

Several children raised their hands and I called on Jonathan. "Twenty-five," he responded correctly.

I planned to have the children figure out how many cubes were in the bowl. Because I wanted to have them deal with a problem that was more unwieldy than doubling 25, I put in additional cubes, two for me and two for each of three other adults—the student teacher, the music teacher, and the regular classroom teacher.

I wrote on the board:

25 children
4 adults

"How many people is that altogether?" I asked them. I gave the children a few minutes to think about the problem and waited until about half the class had raised their hands before asking for responses. I called on Molly first.

"It's 29," she said. "I did it by counting 25, then 26, 27, 28, 29."
I recorded on the board:

Molly   25 … 26, 27, 28, 29

I was pleased that Molly offered her reasoning without being prompted. She had learned that explaining her thinking is part of the process of giving an answer.

"Did anyone figure differently?" I asked.
I called on Leslie. "I knew I had to do 25 plus 4," she began, "and I knew that 5 plus 4 is 9, so I knew that 20 + 9 is 29." I recorded Leslie's explanation numerically under Molly's.

Molly   25 … 26, 27, 28, 29
Leslie   25 + 4
          5 + 4 = 9 so
          20 + 9 = 29

Next I called on Teddy. He told me how to record his idea. "Write 25 and then a 4 underneath," he said. I did so. "Then you move the 4 up to the 5 with an arrow and then you write 29 underneath."

Molly   25 … 26, 27, 28, 29
Leslie   25 + 4
          5 + 4 = 9 so
          20 + 9 = 29
Teddy   25 ↰
           4 ↰
          29

"Did anyone do it a different way?" I asked.
I called on Jason. "I did it like Leslie did," he said.
"Okay," I said. "Does anyone have a new method, one that isn't the same as Molly's, Leslie's, or Teddy's?"
Seth raised his hand. "Mine is like Molly's."
Then Katy called out. "I did it like Molly, too." Several others called out as well.

I called them back to attention and restated my directions. "I'm interested in knowing if there are any different methods I could record on the board," I said. "Raise your hand only if you have a different idea."

Jonathan raised his hand. "Mine's kind of like Leslie's, but it's a little different," he said.

"Tell us about it," I said.

"Well," he said, "I know that 5 plus 2 plus 2 is 9, so I did 25 plus 2 plus 2 is 29."

I added Jonathan's method to the others on the board.

Molly	25 ... 26, 27, 28, 29
Leslie	25 + 4
	5 + 4 = 9 so
	20 + 9 = 29
Teddy	25
	4
	29
Jonathan	5 + 2 + 2 = 9
	25 + 2 + 2 = 29

No one else had a method to explain, so I told them that I would now present a problem for them to figure out. "How many fish are there in the bowl altogether?" I asked.

"What do you mean?" Timmy asked. Timmy is often anxious that he won't be able to do the work.

I restated the problem. "There are two fish in the bowl for each child in the class," I said, "and for four grownups also. The problem is to figure out how many fish there are altogether." I wasn't sure that Timmy understood, but for the moment he seemed reassured.

"Is this a partner or individual problem?" Andrew asked.

Before I could answer, several children gave their opinions.

"Make it partners," Nick said.

"I want to do it alone," Molly said.

"I think we should work together," Jonathan said.

Several others had opinions as well. It was clearly an issue about which many of them had strong feelings. I called them back to attention and told them I was interested in their ideas. I had planned to have them work individually, but I was willing to hear their thoughts, and I was interested in their ideas.

"But you can't call out," I said. "Raise your hand if you want to tell your idea." More than half the class wanted to talk, and I gave all who wanted a turn the chance to speak.

"I think we should work together," Grace said, "because you don't waste time that way."

"It's funner if you have a partner," Rudy said.

"It's better if you do it together," Timmy said, "because you can talk and get help if you need it."

"I like to work alone," Andrew said, "because when I work with some-one, I just tell the answer, and they don't always believe me." Andrew's math ability surpasses his communication skills.

"I don't have a partner," Molly said. Amelia was absent. "But Seth doesn't have one either because Abby isn't here. Can I go sit with Seth?"

"Does that mean you'd rather work with Seth than alone?" I asked. She nodded yes.

"I think we should do it in partners," Leslie said, but she had no reason to offer.

"It's better to work in partners," Nick said, "because you don't have to do all the writing yourself."

As they were talking, I was thinking about what to do. Teaching often requires making decisions on the spot, and it's hard to give an idea careful consideration in the midst of a situation. Generally, I have children work individually when I'm particularly interested in getting a check on their individual abilities. However, I also know that when they're working in pairs I have a chance to assess as I observe and listen to them talk among themselves. I decided that in this case it really didn't matter. I was interested in information about each child's understanding of the 10s and 1s structure of our number system, and I planned to use this activity to assess their understanding, but this part of the lesson was just the introduction to the assessment I'd planned. I collected my thoughts quickly and made a decision.

"Let me tell you how we'll work," I said, and waited for them to quiet down and give me their attention. "There actually are two parts to this problem. I know for sure that I want you to do the second part individually, because it will give me information that will help me know more about your thinking. But, for the first question, it's okay with me if you work alone or with a partner. So it's your choice."

I wrote the problem on the board:

> How many fish are there in the bowl altogether?
> Explain your thinking with numbers and words.
> You can also use pictures.

I also wrote a suggestion for them to use to begin their explanation:

> There are ___ fish in the bowl. I think this because
> _____.

"If you need help beginning your writing," I said, "you can start by copying this."

I continued with further directions. "I'll distribute the paper," I said. "When I come to your table, you tell me whether you're going to work alone or with your partner. If you're working alone, I'll give you your own piece of paper. If you're working together, I'll give you and your partner one piece to use. Decide now."

I walked around the room. Of the 25 students, only 4 decided to work alone. There were 9 pairs and one group of 3. I felt good about how this evolved. I want to support children taking charge of their learning as much

as possible. I was interested in their ideas about working alone or with partners and was interested to see the mode each student chose. It turned out that the two students who had expressed a desire to work alone, Grace and Andrew, wound up working with partners; Maria, who had wanted to work with a partner, chose to work alone. This was the first time I had given the class a choice about how they were to work, and it seemed sensible to me.

Although Sarah and Gwyn worked together, they each used half of the paper for their own solutions. Sarah wrote the numbers from 1 to 29 on a grid and counted them twice. Gwyn added in her head.

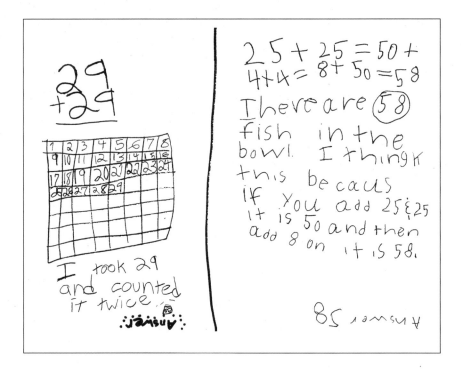

Some children finished more quickly than others. As they completed their papers, I told them to choose an activity from the menu.

Their papers reflected the usual range of responses. Some showed complete understanding of the problem and command over the numbers. Gwyn and Sarah, for example, wrote: *25 + 25 = 50 + 4 + 4 = 8 + 50 = 58. There are 58 fish in the bowl. I think this because if you add 25 & 25 it is 50 and then add 8 on it is 58.* "That's the longest problem I've ever written," Gwyn told me when she gave me the paper. Three other pairs of children and one child who worked alone used this same reasoning.

Rudy and Nick's paper presented a different way of explaining the answer. They wrote: *There are 58 fish in the bowl. We think this because 25 x 2 = 50 and 4 x 2 = 8 and 50 + 8 = 58.* In my experience, using multiplication is unusual for second graders, especially near the beginning of the school year, but Rudy knows a great deal about mathematics. His partners often benefit from his understanding.

Some children relied on a pictorial representation. Teddy and Katy, for example, drew 29 sets of two tallies. They wrote: *We think the ansar is 58 bkas* [because] *we catan* [counted]. Two other pairs of children also made drawings. Tomo and Colleen drew fish; Jonathan and Grace drew 29 trains with two cubes in each.

Teddy and Katy drew tallies in groups of two and counted them.

Five children handed in work that showed their lack of understanding. Since they're free to talk with others, three of these children recorded the correct answer but were not able to offer any explanation, either on their papers or to me orally.

For example, Timmy and Jason weren't able to make sense of the problem, but they discussed it at length and worked hard on their paper. They wrote: *There are 32 fish in the bosl. I think this becuse we counted by 2 we came up 32.*

Eli worked alone. He counted on by writing numbers beginning with 30. He went to 59 but realized he had written one number too many.

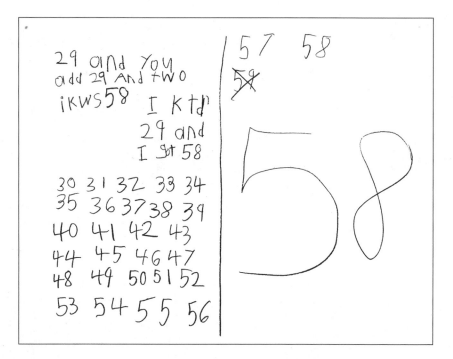

Seth and Andrew worked together and solved the problem symbolically.

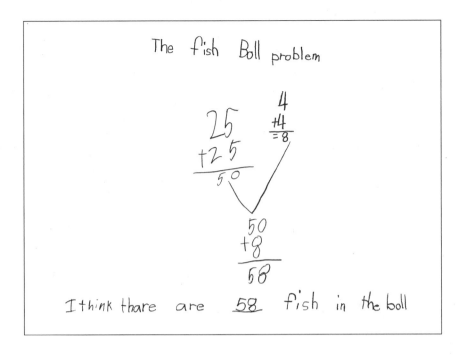

The fish Boll problem

$$25$$
$$+25$$
$$\overline{50}$$

$$4$$
$$+4$$
$$\overline{=8}$$

$$50$$
$$+8$$
$$\overline{58}$$

I think thare are __58__ fish in the boll

Day 2: Counting the Fish

I gathered the children on the rug to talk about their work from the day before. Seeing one another's papers sparked their interest, and a lively discussion resulted about different ways to solve problems and think about numbers. After showing a paper, I asked the children for comments or questions. Also, I asked other questions that occurred to me.

For example, Tomo and Colleen had drawn fish on their paper and also had written a numerical solution: *25 + 25 + 4 + 4.* I asked how they kept track of the fish to know when they had drawn enough. They both looked surprised.

"How many fish did you draw?" I asked.

"I don't know," Tomo said.

"We just decided to draw them," Colleen added.

"Suppose you wanted to draw the actual number of fish," I said, "how could you keep track?"

Tomo shrugged.

"Does anyone have an idea?" I asked.

Timmy raised his hand. "One of you could count while the other draws," he suggested.

"But we both wanted to draw," Colleen said.

"You could each draw some and then write down how many you drew," Molly said.

Sarah had a different suggestion. "One of you could draw for the adults and one for the children," she said.

After we discussed some of their papers, I focused the children once again on the bowl of cubes. "How could we be sure how many fish are in the bowl?" I asked.

"Count them!" they responded in a chorus.

"Since you each put in two cubes, we'll count them by 2s," I said. "But first, let's practice counting by 2s, and I'll record the numbers." As they counted aloud, I listed the numbers on a piece of chart paper. I did this for two reasons. One was that I wanted to have the children examine the patterns of the digits in the sequence of numbers—the repeating pattern of 0, 2, 4, 6, 8 in the ones digits and the pattern of five 1s, five 2s, five 3s, and so on, in the tens digits. Also, I wanted to have the numbers accessible to children who weren't yet sure how to count by 2s. I stopped writing when I reached 58. "Why did I stop here?" I asked.

More than half the hands went up. "I know," Seth said. "Because there are 58 fish."

"How many numbers did I write on this list?" I then asked.

Only a few children raised their hands and they were eager to respond.

"I think there are about 20, or maybe a few more," Nick said.

"That can't be," Andrew blurted out. "There has to be 29 because there were 29 people."

"I don't get it," Maria said.

Sarah raised her hand to explain. "She wrote one number down for each person," she said, "and there are 29 numbers so we got to 58." Sarah was the student who had characterized the problem as 29 + 29.

Maria was still confused. "I still don't get it," she said. Some of the others also seemed confused.

I tried to explain. "I agree with Andrew and Sarah," I said. "I wrote one number for each child and each adult. So the first number could be for your fish, Maria, and the next for Sarah's fish, and the next for Gwyn's, and so on. I put a check mark next to each number as I talked. "I wrote just enough numbers to account for everyone's fish," I concluded.

I wasn't sure my explanation helped. I've become more and more convinced that teaching by telling has a dismal return in terms of helping children learn. I decided to refocus the class on the cubes.

"Let's count the cubes," I said. "I'll set them on the bookcase in 2s and we'll see how many there are."

I had the children count out loud as I put each pair of cubes on the bookcase. I noticed that some of the children were referring to the chart to help them count. We found out that there were 58 cubes.

"Raise your hand if you know how many pairs of cubes I put on the bookcase," I said. I wondered if more children would be able to answer this question because of the concrete context. More than half of the children raised their hands. I called on Amelia.

"There have to be 29 because there was one for each child and each adult," she explained. We counted the pairs to make sure, and I continued with another question.

"If I rearrange the cubes into 5s, then how many trains would there be?" I asked. As I asked the question, I connected two pairs of cubes and added one cube from another pair to make a train with five cubes. I stood it on the bookcase.

No one knew the answer to my question, but I could tell that several were interested and thinking about it. The rest of the class focused on my making trains of five cubes and standing them on the bookcase. The children counted by 5s as I did this.

NOTE Some children do not yet have the developmental maturity to deal with the structure of our number system. They can't think of a digit as representing individual objects in one instance and a group of objects in another. They need time to mature, and while the unit can help their developmental process by providing experiences to stimulate it, their individual learning timetables are a major factor in the development of their understanding.

In the middle of the activity, Teddy called out his discovery. "There will be three extras," he said. "No, maybe four. No, three." Several other children got interested in Teddy's idea and began to chat about it. Although I was curious about Teddy's thinking, I didn't stop to have him explain. I felt it was better to continue with the lesson, as I knew the children would get restless after a while.

Finally, I got to 55 and showed the three remaining cubes. "You were right, Teddy," I said. "There are three extras." He smiled his pleasure.

Grouping by 10s

"I have another question that I'd like you to answer," I then said. "What if we rearranged the cubes again and put them into trains of 10 each? Before we do it, I'm interested in how many trains you think we would have and if you think there would be any extras. If you know, don't call out, but think about a way to explain your idea to others."

For some children, the answer was obvious. Others, however, thought they knew but weren't sure, and some children didn't seem to have any way to think about the problem. My goal was to have those who understood present their ideas so that those who didn't understand would hear a variety of ways to think about the problem. Also, I was curious about how many different ideas the children would generate.

Andrew was eager to report, as always. He was waving his hand with eagerness and insistence. I decided not to call on him. Children are so ready to accept Andrew's thinking that I wanted to give others the chance to offer their ideas first. Having a class discussion like this is hard on Andrew when the problem seems trivial to him.

"I know you're eager to report, Andrew," I said, "but you'll need to wait just a bit. I will call on you, but I'm going to give some other children a chance first." I've learned that this sort of acknowledgment helps with Andrew.

I called on Grace. "Before Grace starts," I said, "I want to remind you to listen carefully to her idea and see if it's different from yours."

"You just count by 10s," Grace said. "You go 10, 20, 30, 40, 50, and then you go 51, 52, 53, 54, 55, 56, 57, 58." She showed with her fingers as she counted.

"So how many 10s and extras are there?" I asked.

Grace needed to count again, and did so quietly to herself, but still using her fingers. Some other children were counting to themselves along with her. "Five 10s and eight more," she finally said.

"I can see that some of you agree," I said. "Does anyone have a different way to think about it?" I called on Sarah.

"I think mine is sort of like Grace's, but a little different," she said.

"Let's hear," I responded.

"Well, I just know that five 10s are 50," she said, "and then it takes eight to go from 50 to 58. So it's five and eight."

"So you agree with Grace," I said. Sarah nodded. I called on Nick next.

"Do you have a different idea?" I asked him.

"It's a little different," he said. "I did 10 plus 10 plus 10 plus 10 plus 10 and that's 50, and then I did 5 plus 3 and that's 8." Nick was pointing to the cubes.

"What do you mean?" Catherine asked.

"Can I show?" Leslie asked. I nodded. She stood up and went over to the bookcase where the cubes were organized into trains of 5. "See, you can push them together and get 10s," she said, but then she got confused. "Then you wouldn't have as many, but I'm not sure how many you'd have. I forgot my idea."

"I can help," Jason said. "Can I?" He looked at me. I nodded and Jason went up to help her.

"It's easy," he said, "you get, like, two for one. Can I move them?" He looked at me for permission. I nodded again. (Jason is a nervous boy who needs approval or reassurance in situations where other children just barrel ahead. I try to be gentle and encouraging with him.) Jason pushed the trains together to make groups with two trains in each.

"Oh, I get it now," Leslie said.

"Why don't you count and see if you get the same answer that Grace and Sarah and Nick did?" I said. Together, Leslie and Jason counted and proved to themselves, and to the class, that there were five 10s and eight extras.

Finally, I called on Andrew. "You just look at the number," he said.

"What do you mean?" I probed.

"You look at the front of 58 and it's a 5," he said. "Then you look at the end and it's 8. So that tells you."

I was pleased with the variety of ideas, but I knew that the children were at different stages of constructing understanding of the relationship of 10s and 1s to our number system. I knew many needed more time and more experience, and I planned to involve the class in similar counting activities on other days.

I planned to repeat this activity later on and have the children each put three, four, or five cubes in the bucket. Also, they would count other things, including pockets and buttons on their clothing, pennies they brought from home, books in the class library, etc.

NOTE A range of understanding and abilities is typical in a class. The activities in this unit are designed to be accessible to children with the least experience and understanding, while offering challenges to those who are more mathematically confident and competent. The unit engages all children in thinking about large numbers, from those children who are just beginning to learn about 10s and 1s to those who fully grasp place value

ASSESSMENT How Many 10s?

FROM THE CLASSROOM

In this assessment, children are asked to report the number of 10s and 1s there are in 58 and explain why their answer makes sense. The number 58 was chosen because the assessment followed the *Counting Fish* whole class lesson and used the number of cubes the children had counted. However, the assessment can be done with any number.

The children's explanations of the number of 10s and 1s are extremely important. Children can learn the pattern that, in a two-digit number, the first digit tells the number of 10s and the second tells the number of 1s. However, being able to recognize that pattern isn't necessarily an indicator that a child understands the meaning of the pattern. Key to a child's understanding of the place value structure of our number system is that the tens' digit tells how many groups of 10 there are, while the ones' digit is a count of individual objects.

Also, note that on the previous day, the class discussed the number of 10s and extras there were in 58. Therefore, figuring out the number of 10s and 1s isn't an issue in this assessment. Rather, the point is for the children to explain the answer. The emphasis for the children is on making sense of the situation and finding a way to convince others. Whether the children know the number of 10s and 1s or have to figure it out, their reasoning process is what is most important for revealing their understanding.

Note: This assessment can also be conducted at the end of the unit to assess the change and growth in children.

"I thought about the class discussion we had yesterday about the number of 10s there were in 58," I said to introduce the assessment. "Today I'm interested in having you do some writing individually. I'm very interested in learning how each of you thinks about figuring out how many 10s and 1s there are in a number. I think that the more I know about how you think, the better I can help each of you learn."

The children were attentive. I think that establishing a real need for their writing helps give them a sense of purpose for the assignment.

"Who can remember how many cubes are in the bowl?" I asked. I waited until more than half the children had raised their hands, and then I called on Hassan.

"58," he said. Others agreed and I recorded the information on the board.

"And who can remember one way we counted the cubes in the bowl?" I then asked. I waited and called on Nick.

"First we did it by 2s," he said. "There were 29 and we got 58." I recorded this as well and called on Katy.

"We did it by 5s, too," she said.

"And there were three extras," Teddy blurted out. Teddy has the tendency to blurt out. I've talked to him about it and he's become more aware of the problem. He put his hand quickly to his mouth, a gesture that showed me he was aware of what he had done. I chose not to comment on it.

"Yes, there were three extra cubes," I said. "Does anyone remember how many trains of five there were?" I called on Marina.

"There were 11 and 3 extra," she said. Others nodded their agreement. I added this information on the board.

Many children were eager to offer more information. I called on Molly, pleased that she had her hand raised. She's a dreamy child whose attention often wanders during class discussions.

"We did it by 10s," she said, "and there were five of them with eight left over." I recorded this on the board as well. I had written:

> There are 58 cubes in the bowl.
> We counted by 2s. There were 29 2s.
> We counted by 5s. There were 11 5s and 3 extras.
> We counted by 10s. There were 5 10s and 8 extras.

"Listen as I explain what I'd like you to write," I said. "You are to write an explanation to convince someone that there were five 10s and eight extras when we made trains of 10. Yesterday, there were different ideas about how you thought about this. Today, you have to pick one of those ideas that made sense to you and write about it."

"How do we do it?" Maria asked.

"I'll write a suggestion on the board for how you might begin your recording," I said. "Remember to be sure to use numbers and words and, if you want, pictures."

I wrote on the board:

> There are ___ 10s in 58 and ___ extras.
> I think this because _____ .

"Can I have a harder question?" Andrew asked, with a tone of slight exasperation. There was a typically wide range of mathematical ability and experience in the class, from four children who knew little about numbers to Andrew and several others whose understanding was impressive. To respond to Andrew's request, I wrote an additional challenge on the board:

> How many 9s are there in 58? Explain.

I gave one last direction. "The trains are where we left them yesterday," I said, "so you can go and refer to them if you'd like." I distributed paper and they got to work.

The children jumped into the task. Because we had discussed the problem the day before, children were familiar with it and, therefore, more comfortable with this assignment. Also, I think they were getting generally more comfortable with writing.

Some children drew pictures, either of cubes or of tally marks. Jonathan typically draws tally marks to help him think about numbers. In this case, he drew 58 tallies in groups of 5 and wrote: *There are 5 10s in 58 and 8 extras. I think this because I cantid the tens and cantid the extras.*

Jonathan resorted to drawing tallies, his pre-ferred method for making sense of numbers.

> There are 5 10s in 58 and
> 8 extras I think this because
> I cantid the tens and cantid the extras.
> ||| ||| ||| ||| ||| ||| ||| ||| ||| |||

Even though his writing skills were poor, Eli's paper revealed his mathe-matical reasoning. He first copied the prompt from the board. However, it didn't seem to make sense to him and he ignored it and wrote his own sentence: *There are 5 10s and 8 are left.* He brought his paper to me.

"How do you know there are five 10s?" I asked.

"What do you mean?" he asked.

"Your paper doesn't explain how you figured it out," I said.

"What should I do?" he asked.

"More words," I suggested, "or a picture, or both." Eli returned to his seat. On the bottom of his paper, he drew 10 trains with five cubes in each. He circled groups of two trains, labeled each *1 10,* and began to write. Because he started writing near the bottom of his paper, he ran out of room. That didn't bother Eli at all, however, and he concluded his state-ment up near the middle of the page. I was confused when I saw his paper, but when Eli read it to me, it made sense. He read, "All the two 10s equals 40. If you add one more 10 it equals 50 and there will be 8 more left so it will be 58." What he had written on his paper was: *al the 2 10s ekws = 40 if you add wun mor 10 it ekws 50 and ther will be 8 mor left so it will be 58.* I accepted Eli's paper, deciding that this wasn't the best time or place to work on his writing.

Eli's work reveals his math thinking but shows the need for more work on his writing.

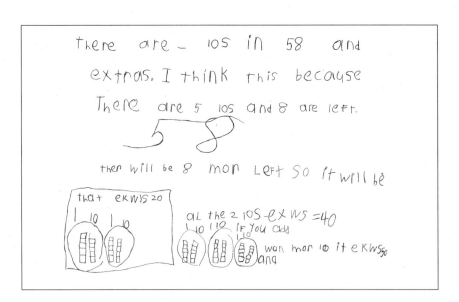

Other children described their thinking without pictures. Amelia, for example, wrote: *There are 58 fish. We counted by 2s. We counted by 5s. But every way we counted we allways got 58. There are 5 ten's in 58 and there are 8 extras. I thingk this because if you counted by ten's & you counted 5 times you wad [would] endup with 50 but sen's there are 58 and then there are 8 extras then it = 58.*

Amelia is a prolific writer and enjoys explaining her math discoveries.

> There are 58 fish
>
> We Counted by 2s.
> We Counted by 5s. But eVery
> Way We Counted We
> allways got 58.
> there are 5 ten's ih 58 and
> There are 8 extras. I thingk this
> because
> if you counted by ten's & you
> Counted 5 time's you Wad ehdup
> With 5o but Sen's there are
> 58 and then there are 8 extras
> then it = 58.

Hassan wrote: *There are 5 10s in 58 and 8 extras. I think this because 1 is 10 2 is 20 3 is 30 4 is 40 5 is 50 8 extras.*

Hassan's math understanding surpasses his ability to communicate in writing.

> there are 5 10s in 58 and
> 8 extras. I think this because
> 1 is 10 2 is 20 3 is 30
> 4 is 40 5 is 05
> 8 extras.

NOTE One piece of work isn't sufficient for judging a child's understanding. A collection of evidence is necessary to compile an informative and accurate picture of a child's mathematical ability. From working with students in class, reading their written assignments, observing them at work, listening to their comments in class discussions, and talking with them individually, teachers can form a detailed impression of children's understanding.

After figuring out how many 10s and 1s there were in 58, Andrew figured out how many 9s and 1s there were.

Rudy gave the explanation that Andrew had given in class. He wrote: *There are 5 tens in 58 and 8 extras. I think this because you look at the beging of 58 and it's a 5. then you look at the ending and it's a 8. and thats wi* [why] *I think that.* Rudy's statement on this paper doesn't, by itself, guarantee his understanding. From Rudy's other classwork, however, I know that he fully grasps the relationship of 10s and 1s to our number system.

Teddy thought about the problem in a way that was new to me. He started with 58 and subtracted 10s to get 48, 38, 28, 18, and 8. He counted to find he used 5 tens and still had 8 left.

Four children had no idea about how to think about the question. Catherine, for example, wrote: *I donun't get this.* She needed many more experiences to construct understanding of our number system.

As I had done with their solutions to the number of fish in the bowl, I gathered the children for a discussion and had some of them present their work. We discussed the different ways they displayed their thinking.

Note: Andrew was the only child who did the challenge of figuring out how many groups of 9 and extras there would be in 58 cubes. To solve the problem, he drew tallies and organized them into 10s by circling two groups of five. Then he moved one tally from each group of 10 to make them groups of 9. He wound up with six groups of 9 and four extras and wrote: *There are 6 nines and 4 ones.*

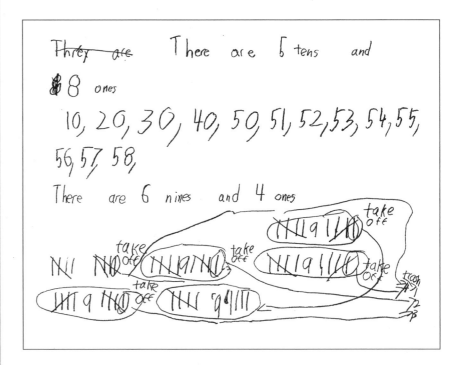

WHOLE CLASS LESSON   The King's Commissioners

Overview

The King's Commissioners by Aileen Friedman provides an imaginary context to present the same sort of problem as *Counting Fish*. (See page 56.) In the story, 47 king's commissioners are counted by 2s, 5s, and 10s. The lesson asks students to make sense of different ways of counting, offering them another opportunity to see the relationship between groups of 10 and the numbers that represent them. This lesson is appropriate for later in the unit, after children have had a variety of grouping and counting experiences.

Before the lesson

Gather these materials:
■ *The King's Commissioners* by Aileen Friedman (See Children's Books section, page 169.)

Teaching directions

■ Read the book to the class. In the story, the King wants to know how many commissioners he has. His two Royal Advisors count the commissioners in different ways. One counts by 2s and reports that there are 23 2s and 1 extra; the other counts by 5s and reports 9 5s and 2 extras. Their methods confuse the King, who wants only to know the total number of commissioners. The Princess steps in to help. She has the commissioners line up in rows of 10, counts four rows of 10 with 7 left over, and convinces the King that there are 47 in all. She proceeds to explain why the Royal Advisors' methods were also correct.

Stop reading before the Princess steps in and after the Royal Advisors have reported. Ask the students how many commissioners they think there are and have volunteers explain their reasoning. Then finish the story.

■ Begin a class discussion of the story. On the board, write the numbers that show how the Royal Advisors and the Princess counted:

$$23 \text{ 2s and 1 extra}$$
$$9 \text{ 5s and 2 extra}$$
$$10 \text{ 4s and 7 extra}$$

Ask: Why was the King confused? What did he mean when he kept saying, "That doesn't tell me anything"? How can you explain why the First Royal Advisor was correct? Why was the Second Royal Advisor also correct? Why was the Princess's method easy for the King to understand?

On the board, you may want to draw the tally marks as the Royal Advisors did.

■ To prepare children for the writing assignment, again ask them to explain why the First Royal Advisor's answer of 23 2s and 1 extra made sense. As students explain, record their thinking numerically on the board to model ways to represent children's ideas with mathematical symbolism.

■ Give the writing assignment of explaining why each counting method in the story made sense. Write the following prompts on the board:

1. The First Royal Advisor made sense because _____.
2. The Second Royal Advisor made sense because _____.
3. The Princess made sense because _____.

■ As children finish their work, have them bring it to you and read it aloud. If you have time, use this opportunity to conduct informal assessments. Ask: "Suppose there were 54 commissioners instead of 47. If the Princess lined them up in 10s, how many rows and extras would there be?" Note which children see the question as trivial, which need to think before answering, and which aren't able to figure it out.

■ On the next day, return to the story by reminding the children about the King's comment at the end of the book about the number of commissioners: "'That's not so many,' he said. 'We can still have more.'" Ask children to think of other commissioners the King might appoint and how many he might need. You may want to list the children's estimates on the board or even graph them. Pick several of the numbers suggested and have students discuss how many rows and extras there would be if those numbers represented commissioners that the Princess lined up in 10s.

■ Optional: Present another writing assignment. Have children list other commissioners the King might appoint, then explain how many he would have altogether and how many rows and extras he would have if they all lined up in 10s. I chose to make this assignment optional for the children.

FROM THE CLASSROOM

I told the class the title of the book and asked if they knew what commissioners did. Several had ideas.

"They work for the police," Jason said, "doing investigations and things."

"They take care of stuff in offices," Leslie said.

"They're like the king's men," Nick said.

"I think they're something royal," Andrew said.

"Let's see what you think after you hear the story," I said.

After I read how the two Royal Advisors kept track of the commissioners and reported to the King, Tomo's and Andrew's hands shot up. Several children began talking to one another. I stopped reading and called on Tomo.

"I know it," he said, excitedly. "It's 47."

"How did you figure that out?" I asked.

"I did 5, 10, 15, 20, 25, 30, 35, 40, 45, and then 2 more is 47," he said. He had used his fingers to be sure he counted nine 5s.

"I got the same thing," Andrew said. "I did it the same way."

"What about the First Royal Advisor?" I asked. "He had reported 23 2s. Is that 47 also?" Neither of the boys or any of the other children knew. Somehow, 23 seemed like too many 2s to work with.

I continued reading the story. The Princess decided to arrange the commissioners into rows of 10 and organized them into four rows with seven

commissioners left over. Before the Princess counted by 10s, about half of the children figured out that there were 47 commissioners in all.

I asked the children if they had any comments about the story.

"I liked the things the commissioners did," Seth said.

"I think that there should be a Commissioner for Messy Rooms," Sarah said.

"I don't think the King was a very good King," Nick commented.

"Why not?" I asked.

"He didn't know very much," Nick responded.

Teddy jumped in. "You can't really tell if he's a good king from the story. Maybe he just wasn't good in math."

"But he's a grownup," Amelia said.

"Why do you think the King was confused?" I then asked, trying to turn the conversation toward some mathematical thinking. This question didn't help, however.

"He didn't know how many commissioners he had," Colleen said.

"He had too many people working for him, and he didn't know what they all did," Teddy offered.

"He didn't remember what he learned in school," Katy added.

I then asked a different question to elicit responses about the counting. "The Princess said that the two Royal Advisors were correct," I said. The children nodded their agreement.

"How could you prove that the First Royal Advisor was right when he reported 23 2s and 1 extra?" I asked. I gave them a few moments to think about this, taking the time to draw tally marks on the board to show 23 groups of two and 1 extra. By then, about eight of the children had raised their hands. I called on Teddy.

|| || || || || || || || || ||

|| || || || || || || || || ||

|| || || |

"You count by 2s to 20," he began. "And that uses up 10 of them. Then another 10 is 20 and 20 plus 20 is 40. Then you go 2 plus 2 plus 2 plus 1 equals 7. So it's 47."

"Let me see if I can write down what you explained," I said. I often record the children's explanations numerically to model for them how mathematical symbolism can be used to describe their thinking. I wrote on the board, verifying with Teddy as I did so:

Count by 2s to 20 (10 2s)
20 + 20 = 40 (20 2s)
2 + 2 + 2 + 1 = 7
40 + 7 = 47

"Does anyone have a different way to prove that 23 2s and 1 extra equals 47?" I asked. I called on Molly.

"I figured that 23 plus 23 is 46," she reported, "and 1 more makes 47." I recorded on the board:

$$23 + 23 = 46$$
$$46 + 1 = 47$$

"How come you decided to add 23 and 23?" I probed.

"Because you have 23 two times," she said, referring to the 23 groups of tally marks on the board.

"Does anyone have a different way?" I asked. I called on Grace.

"First I did five 2s," she said. "I made a bundle and it has 10." Grace showed a piece of paper on which she had drawn tally marks and a loop around groups of five 2s.

"Then I made more bundles the same size," she continued, "so I had four bundles and that's 10, 20, 30, 40. Then I did the three 2s and the 1 more and it's 47 all together." I made loops around the tally marks on the board to show the class what Grace had done on her paper.

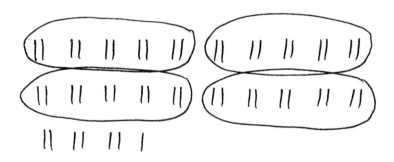

I also wrote:

$$5 \ 2s = 10$$
$$10, 20, 30, 40, \text{ and } 3 \ 2s \text{ and } 1 \text{ more} = 47$$

"Does anyone have another idea?" I asked again. Nick raised his hand. "Mine is kind of like Grace's," he said.

"Tell us," I responded. I then told the class, "Be sure to listen carefully to see if Nick's idea is the same as Grace's idea."

"I did five 2s," he began, "and then I did five more and that was 10 2s and that was 20. Then I did 20 and 20 is 40, and that used up 20 2s. Then I counted the 7 and got 47." I wrote:

$$5 \ 2s = 10$$
$$10 \ 2s = 20$$
$$20 + 20 = 40 + 7 = 47$$

NOTE Continuing to ask the class for other ways to explain reinforces the idea that there is more than one way to think about a problem. Also, it encourages children to keep thinking when someone else offers a correct solution or explanation and to search for new and different approaches.

"Any other ideas?" I asked. I called on Rudy.

"I have a trick," he said. "I know 2 and 2 is 4, so I know that 20 and 20 is 40, and then you go 42, 44, 46, 47." I wrote:

$$2 + 2 = 4, 20 + 20 = 40$$
$$42, 44, 46, 47$$

"Any more ideas?" I asked. There were none.

A Writing Assignment

"You'll each do some writing now about the story and the math thinking," I said. "There are three parts."

"First, you explain one of the ways to prove that the First Royal Advisor was correct," I said. "You can use one of the ways on the board, or any other way you want. Here is how you can start your writing." I wrote on the board:

1. The First Royal Advisor made sense because _____.

I explained the other two parts. "Then you'll do the same for the Second Royal Advisor and the Princess. Watch as I write how you can start writing for each." I wrote on the board:

2. The Second Royal Advisor made sense because _____.
3. The Princess made sense because _____.

"What do we use for a title?" Seth asked, always concerned about being correct. I usually give the children a title for their papers, but I decided to listen to their ideas. I was curious to know how the story had stimulated their imaginations.

"What do you think would be a good title?" I asked the class.

"How about 'Counting for the King'?" Sarah said.

"I think 'How Many Commissioners?'" Abby suggested.

"Maybe 'It Made Sense,'" Hassan said.

"I'll let you each decide," I told the class. "It will be okay if you have different titles."

I gave one last direction. "Remember," I said, "you must use words and numbers on your paper and, if you'd like, pictures." Several of the children said "pictures" with me. They'd heard me give this direction many times for writing assignments.

The children got to work with the typical confusion that erupts when I give a writing assignment. Writing is difficult for some children, and I need to do a great deal of encouraging and prodding to get them all started and to keep them going. Sometimes it feels like trying to keep a dozen or more balloons in the air. I persist, however, not only because writing helps children clarify their mathematical reasoning but also because their written work provides me with evidence of their thinking and reasoning.

Katy tried to explain each of the three methods.

> The Kings commissioners
> the first Royal advisor Made sense
> because He got the nemder
> (11) (11) (11) (11) (11) (11) (11) (11)
> (11) (11) (11) (11) (11) (11) (11) (11)
> (11) (11) (11) (11) (11) (11) (11) 1
> the second Royal adisor Made
> sens because 9 5s + 2 more
> = 47 ~~卌 卌 卌 卌 卌~~
> 卌 卌 卌 卌 11
> the princess Made sense
> because all thos 10s
> wod Make 47 10 10
> 10 10 7

Hassan's math ability surpasses his writing ability. He turned 9 5s to 5 9s and added 18 + 18 + 9 to get 45.

> The Big uh-oh
>
> The First Royal Advisor made
> sense because: 2 3 2s=46
> 23+23=46 46 15 46+1=47
> The second Royal Advisr made sense
> because: 9 5s and 2 more
> 18+18+9 = 45 +2 = 47.
> The princess made sense becaue!
> 10+10+10+10+7=47

Molly still has difficulty with reversals when she writes numerals.

> It mad sens
>
> 1 The first royal advisor made sense because: 23+ 23=46 46+1=47
>
> 2. The second Royal Advisor made sense because (IIIII)5+5=10 (IIIII)10+5=15 (IIIII)15+5=20 (IIIII) 20+5=25 (IIIII)25+5=30 (IIIII)30+5=35 (IIIII)35+5=40 (IIIII)40+5=45. 45+2=47
>
> The prinsess madesense becacse: 4 10s=40 40+7=47

Informal Assessment

As each child brought his or her paper to me, I posed another problem. For example, I said to Tomo, "Suppose there were 54 commissioners instead of 47. If the Princess lined them up in 10s, how many rows and extras would there be?"

The problem was trivial for Tomo. Without hesitation, he answered, "Five rows and four extras." Amelia, Molly, Rudy, Leslie, and Nick answered similarly.

Andrew gave an extra explanation. "The number tells you," he said. "The 5 means five rows and the 4 means four extras." Andrew's understanding of place value is solid.

About half the class gave correct responses but took time to figure it out. Katy, for example, counted by 10s on her fingers before reporting that there would be five rows and four extras.

Five of the children didn't have any idea or any way to think about the number of 10s and extras in 54. When I asked Colleen, for example, she just shrugged. On her paper, she had ignored the prompts I had put on the board and had written 47 ones: *1 + 1 + 1 + ...* Actually, I doubted that there were exactly 47 ones, as Colleen frequently miscounts.

I took Colleen's paper and asked her a question. "Suppose there were only 15 commissioners," I said, "and the Princess lined them up in 10s. How many rows do you think there would be?"

Colleen thought for a minute and shrugged again.

"Do you think there are enough commissioners to make a row of 10?" I asked. Colleen immediately nodded.

"Do you think there are enough to make two rows of 10?" I continued.

Colleen thought for a minute. "Maybe," she said, "I'm not sure."

"I have an idea," I said. "Would you go over and count out 15 Snap Cubes and take them to your desk?" Colleen nodded eagerly. "Then come and get me, and we'll see if there are enough for one row of 10 or more."

At this time, I didn't demand more from Colleen's writing. She needs to work with smaller quantities first.

Timmy was another child who didn't know how many rows and extras there would be with 47 commissioners. Timmy has a difficult time focusing on activities and writing. When he brought his paper to me, it had only his name, the date, and a title: *The king count.*

"I don't know what to write," he said. I've learned that referring Timmy to the prompts on the board doesn't help him. And I didn't want to focus him on the writing before we had a chance to talk about the mathematics.

I gave Timmy the same problem I gave to Colleen. "Suppose there were only 15 commissioners," I said, "and the Princess lined them up in 10s. How many rows do you think there would be?"

"That's easy," Timmy said. "She could make one row and there would be five more."

"Why is 15 so easy for you?" I asked.

Timmy thought for a minute. "It just is," he said.

"What about if there were 23 commissioners?" I asked.

"Oooh, that's harder," he responded. "Oh, I know, 10 and 10 are 20 with 3 left over. Oh, I get it." Timmy got excited and continued.

"I know how to do 47," he said, "You go 10, 20, 30, 40." He didn't complete the thought but took his paper and went back to work. Timmy still didn't follow the directions for the complete assignment, but he wrote about what he understood.

NOTE It's important to remember that the primary goal of a lesson is not to have children write but to have them think and reason. Writing can serve as a tool for children to explore their thinking or as a record of the ideas they've already formulated. But the emphasis must be kept, first and foremost, on their thinking. The written product provides a record of their ideas. Teachers need to make decisions about when to push for written evidence, when to accept oral evidence, and when to push for both.

Timmy wrote only about the Princess, explaining the benefit of grouping by 10s.

> The king count
> I liked the princess iday
> because she coned by tens.
> I think that is the eseist whay
> to count. She put the commissioners
> in tens. There where 47 guys
> counted them 4 tens plus
> 7 that = 47.

After talking with a few more children, I went to check on Colleen. She was putting 15 cubes together in trains, sorting them by color. "Let's pretend these are commissioners," I said to her. Colleen nodded.

"Can you make a row of 10?" I asked. She nodded again and picked up a train of four red cubes and a train of three yellow cubes. She snapped

them together and counted them. Then she added a train of four green cubes and counted again. When she got to 11, she removed one cube and looked at me.

"How many in that train?" I asked.

"Ten?" she said, tentatively, and then counted them again.

"So if the Princess lined up the commissioners in 10s, these 10 would be in one row," I said. Colleen nodded.

"Do you have enough for another row?" I asked.

Colleen counted the extras and said, "No, there are only five more."

"So with 15 commissioners," I said, "there's one row of 10 and five extras. Could you do the same with 47 cubes?"

"Maybe," Colleen responded.

By now, however, it was time for lunch. I told Colleen to put away the cubes for now, and I asked the class to get ready for lunch dismissal.

Day 2: Extending the Story

I began class the next day by reminding the children about the King's comment at the end of the story after he was convinced there were 47 commissioners. "'That's not so many,' he said. 'We can still have more.'"

"What other commissioners do you think he could have?" I asked the class. The children had a wide range of ideas. Some seemed to think of their personal or classroom needs and suggested commissioners for cleaning out pet tanks, sharpening pencils, dirty socks, brushing hair, making breakfast, bad cuts, and more. Some ideas seemed to be related to how the children perceived the King's needs, such commissioners for crown cleaning, putting the Princess to bed, and cutting beards. Nick, who is more savvy than most of the children about the world at large, suggested that there be a commissioner for Elvis sightings.

The children were eager to continue talking about the different jobs for commissioners, but I wanted to direct the class discussion toward some mathematical thinking. "You have lots of ideas," I said, "and I'm interested in giving you more time to think about them. But right now I want to ask another question."

Eli raised his hand. "I think one should be for kicking out the cook if the food isn't good," he said. The children laughed, and others began to raise their hands.

"Please put your hands down and listen," I said, quieting the class. "I will give you more time to think about commissioners and to write about your ideas and draw some pictures, if you like. But now I'd like you to think about a different question."

When I had the children's attention, I asked, "How many commissioners do you think the King should have? Think about this for a moment, and when you have an idea, raise your hand."

The children's estimates ranged from Colleen's suggestion of 10 commissioners to Andrew's 347. Most of their numbers ranged from the 20s through the 60s.

Molly reported her answer in a different way. "I think the King needs eight more commissioners," she said, "one for taking pictures, two for cleaning, and a couple more."

To avoid letting the discussion shift to what the commissioners might do, I asked the class, "If the King appointed eight more commissioners, and he had 47 already, how many would he have altogether? Talk to your partner about this."

The room buzzed with conversation. Many children used their fingers to count. Two children went to the 0–99 chart to figure. After a few minutes, I called the class to attention.

"Since it was Molly's suggestion, I'll let her report," I said.

"It's 55," she said, and explained using her fingers. "I went 48, 49, 50, 51, 52, 53, 54, 55, 56, 57, 58." Other children nodded.

I wrote 55 on the board. "Now my question is this," I said. "If the Princess lined up the 55 commissioners, how many rows would there be and how many extras?"

A few children immediately raised their hands. I waited a minute and a few more children raised their hands. Children reported the same sorts of methods they used when I'd asked them the question individually the day before. I took the time to allow as many different students to report as wanted to. I find that when students explain their thinking, they not only cement their own ideas but they also offer their classmates different ideas.

I then gave the children two options. "You can either choose a task from the menu," I said, "or write about other commissioners the King could appoint and how many he would have altogether."

Annie added 20 more commissioners.

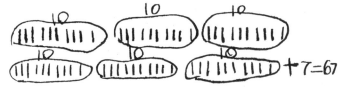

On this paper, Timmy was able to explain
how he grouped 33 into 10s and extras.

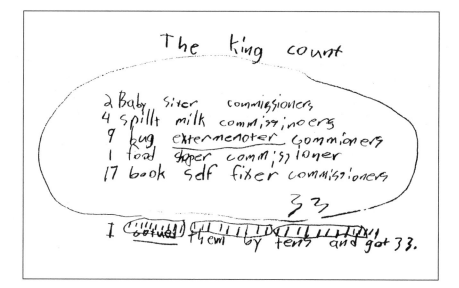

Sarah thought the King would need 10
more commissioners, but she didn't explain
how many 10s and 1s there would be.

CONTENTS

Race for $1.00   92
Dollar Signs   101
Cover a Flat   110
0–99 Patterns   122
Number Puzzle   129
Fill the Cube   134
Make a Shape   146
Five Tower Game   152
Guess My Number   160

MENU ACTIVITIES

The activities on the menu were selected to offer children a variety of ways to think about the place value structure of our number system. The menu was constructed with the consideration that not all children engage with or experience activities in the same way; it includes activities that appeal to different interests and aptitudes. Although you can require students to do all of the menu activities, expect children to respond differently. This is to be expected and respected. Also, the activities are intended to be revisited over and over, and the menu gives children the opportunity to return to those that especially interest them.

Three of the menu activities extend the whole class lessons. *Dollar Signs* offers a different context for the *Stars in One Minute* lesson. *0–99 Patterns* and *Number Puzzle* extend children's experiences with *The 0–99 Chart* lesson. And *Make a Shape, Five Tower Game,* and *Fill the Cube* all provide experiences based on *Counting Fish.*

An assortment of materials is used for some of the menu activities. Pennies, dimes, and play dollars are needed for *Race for $1.00,* a game that offers a real-life application of our place value system. *Cover a Flat* is a game that is similar to *Race for $1.00,* but it uses Base Ten Blocks instead of money and offers children a different visual perspective on place value. Color Tiles, Snap Cubes, and Unifix cubes are used for *Make a Shape, Five Tower Game,* and *Fill the Cube.* These three activities engage children with counting large numbers of objects while providing experiences with measuring area, length, and volume.

The remaining activity, *Guess My Number,* doesn't require any materials. It's a game in which children identify guesses as greater or less than a secret number.

Menu activities that require students to work in pairs are marked with a "P" in the upper right-hand corner; those that can be done individually are marked with an "I." Also, check page 5 for suggestions about organizing the menu activities and materials.

FROM THE CLASSROOM

"Talk with your partner," I said to the children at the beginning of math class one day. "When you've both agreed on the activity you'd like to do, raise your hands." With this direction, I began a day of work on menu activities with my second grade class. During "menu" time, students are free to choose the activities they'd like to do. I had already introduced four of the nine independent menu activities in the unit and given the class portions of several periods to become familiar with them.

This was the end of the second week of the Place Value unit. During the first two weeks, I taught two whole class lessons to the children, spending three days on The *0-99 Chart* lesson and four days on *Stars in One Minute.* Before beginning the unit, I organized the children into pairs by having them randomly draw playing cards. For storing their work, I made each child a folder from construction paper, put the folders in alphabetical order, and numbered them so they were easy to keep organized. Also, I prepared a list of the menu activities for children to keep in their folders.

Today, Gwyn had distributed the folders before class began. She enjoys organizational chores and often helps with them in the class. I gave the children time to talk with their partners and choose activities. I then asked for their attention and called on Hassan and Catherine first.

"Race for $1.00," they responded in unison.

"Who will get the materials?" I asked.

They looked at each other. "I will," Hassan answered. This seemed fine with Catherine. One part of my class system is that only one child is needed to get the materials. This cuts down on the traffic near the shelves where the math materials are kept.

"Don't forget to take a copy of the directions," I reminded Hassan. Multiple copies of the directions for each activity are available for students to use. Many do not like to refer to them, but I encourage it. Not only is the reading good practice, but it cuts down on the number of questions they address to me.

Next I called on Katy and Teddy. "We'll do *Race for $1.00,"* Katy said, "and Teddy will get the stuff." I nodded and called on Corrine and Eli.

"We'll do the one with the stopwatch," Corrine said.

"Which activity is that?" I asked.

"I don't know the name," she said.

"Look at the list," I said, "and find the name of the activity you'd like to do." She and Eli scanned the list but couldn't find it.

"Who can help them?" I asked.

"Dollar Signs," several children called out.

I looked at Corrine and Eli. *"Dollar Signs,"* they answered together, nodding. I told them that one of them should get the materials and the directions.

I then called on Rudy and Nick. Nick complained, "He wants to do *Cover a Flat,* but I want to do the individual one." Each task is marked with a "P" or and "I" to indicate whether partners are needed or whether a child can work on it individually. It's okay for pairs to work together on individual activities, but they each have to do their own recording. Three of the menu activities I had introduced so far called for a partner, and one could be done individually.

"You'll have to find a way to decide," I said. I don't solve these sorts of problems for children, unless I feel they've gone as far as they can and can't come to a resolution. Then I meet with them to discuss the problem and help them come to a decision. Also, from time to time I have class discussions in which students report the different ways they've found to resolve conflicts in choices. Typically, they find some way to choose, often by playing a game like *Scissors, Paper, Rock* or by having one child hide an object in one hand and the other guess which hand it's in. Sometimes children agree to spend part of the class time on one activity and part on another. Although making these decisions eats into their math time, I think the time is well spent because I've seen children's abilities to cooperate and negotiate improve greatly.

Nick and Rudy decided to play *Cover a Flat* for half the time and then do *0–99 Patterns.* They were now talking about what time it would be when half the time was over. I let them continue their discussion.

Next I called on Maria and Timmy. "We're going to do *Dollar Signs* like Eli and Corrine," Timmy said. They were having difficulty making a choice, but when Eli and Corrine, who sat across from them, decided on *Dollar Signs,* they chose it also. Timmy got up to get the stopwatch and the directions; Maria went to get paper.

I continued letting the students make choices. One problem arose when all six baggies of money for *Race for $1.00* had been claimed, and Gwyn and Sarah wanted to play the game.

"You'll have to make another choice for now," I said. "When another pair finishes playing, you can switch activities if you'd like." The girls chose to do *0–99 Patterns* and work together. Sarah went to get the directions and the patterns.

Seth and Abby were also disappointed about not being able to play *Race for $1.00.* They decided to play *Cover a Flat,* and Seth went for supplies. By this time, Nick and Rudy had negotiated the halfway time, and Nick went to get the materials for *Cover a Flat.*

Finally, all the children had chosen their activities. This procedure took just about 10 minutes. Six pairs of children were playing *Race for $1.00,* clearly that day's favorite; three pairs had chosen *Dollar Signs;* two pairs were playing *Cover a Flat;* one pair and Andrew working alone were investigating *0–99 Patterns.* Math time was underway. The room was noisy but not unruly, and everyone was engaged.

Children's Responses

As the children worked on the menu tasks, I circulated and supervised. This was the first day I was devoting entirely to the menu. On previous days, I had spent part of each period introducing an activity or following up on the whole class lessons before the children could get to what they called their "work."

As I circulated, I interacted with children in different ways. Sometimes I helped children understand the activity or some aspect of the mathematics involved. Sometimes I had to refocus children on tasks or help them negotiate differences. Sometimes I posed questions to children to help me assess their understanding. And at times I merely took note of what students were doing and listened to their conversations without interrupting.

Race for $1.00 is one of five two-person games on the menu. When introducing all of these games, I tell the students that these are games to "play and see what happens" rather than "games to play and see who wins." In this way, I shift the emphasis from competition to mathematical thinking. For example, after teaching the rules for *Race for $1.00,* I say to the children, "You'll have the chance to play this game many times and, most likely, you'll each get $1.00 first in some of the games. What's most important to me is that you pay attention to each other as you take your turns, try and keep track of who has more and less money, and try to think about how much more you need to get to $1.00."

Leslie and Jason were playing *Race for $1.00.* "Who's ahead?" I asked. They didn't know.

"Can you figure it out?" I asked. They counted their dimes and pennies and reported their amounts. Leslie had 32 cents and Jason had 27.

"She has more," Jason said. They both grinned and returned to their game. I watched as Jason rolled a 6 and a 4 and counted on his fingers to get 10. He reached for pennies.

"Why don't you just take a dime?" Leslie asked.

"Oh, yeah," Jason said. He stopped counting pennies, added a dime to his pile, and said, "Now I think I'm ahead." He gave the dice to Leslie.

Tomo rushed across the room to me. He and Colleen were also playing *Race for $1.00.* "We've run out of pennies," he said, tugging on my shirt sleeve. I've come to know that the tugging is a sign that Tomo is frustrated. I went to their table and saw that Colleen had a pile of pennies.

"She won't exchange," Tomo said.

"I don't want to," Colleen said.

"Do you know how many pennies are worth the same as one dime?" I asked her. Colleen shook her head no.

"I know," Tomo said, "it's 10."

"That's right," I said. "If you exchange 10 pennies for one dime, you'll still have the same amount of money."

"Okay," Colleen said, reluctantly. I don't think she was convinced, but she went along with the game.

Molly and Amelia were also playing *Race for $1.00.* I watched Molly roll a 6 and a 3 and then respond in a way that is mathematically sophisticated for a second grader. She added the numbers quickly in her head, took a penny from the pile of money she already had, returned it to the baggie, and took one dime. She did this quickly and effortlessly.

"Was that okay with you?" I asked Amelia. Amelia had watched Molly but hadn't said anything. She remained silent for a moment.

"Oh, I get it," she then said. "She did it backwards."

"What do you mean?" I probed.

"Well," she answered, "she did like a shortcut. Instead of taking all the pennies and then exchanging, she made believe she took the pennies."

"Is that what you did?" I asked Molly.

"I don't know," she said. "I just did it." I left the girls to continue their game.

Three pairs of students were engaged in *Dollar Signs*. From their experience drawing stars for one minute in the whole class lesson, the students were comfortable with this activity. Maria showed me her paper when I walked by the table where she and Timmy sat. "I counted the dollar signs by 1s and 2s," she told me, "and I got 27."

"Suppose you counted by 10s," I said to Maria, "how many 10s would there be?" She didn't know. Neither did Timmy. I asked them to try and figure it out.

"Let me know when you've got an answer," I said. "I'm interested in what you'll find out."

Andrew came up. "I'm working on my third 0–99 pattern," he said. He did not have a partner that day and was content to explore other children's patterns on the 0–99 chart. Andrew is usually drawn to the more abstract activities.

Andrew worked individually and created another 0–99 pattern.

0–99 Chart

0	1	2	3	4	5	6	X	8	9
10	11	12	13	14	15	16	X	18	19
20	21	22	23	24	25	26	X	28	29
30	31	32	33	34	35	36	X	38	39
40	41	42	43	44	45	46	X	48	49
50	51	52	53	54	55	56	X	58	59
60	61	62	63	64	65	66	X	68	69
▓	X	X	X	X	X	X	▓	X	X
80	81	82	83	84	85	86	X	88	89
90	91	92	93	94	95	96	X	98	99

All numbers that start or end with seven.

"Can I make up new patterns?" he asked. "That would be fine," I said. "If you give them to me, I'll add them to the class set."

Abby and Seth were playing *Cover a Flat* and had a question. "How many of the little cubes make a tens rod?" they asked.

"How could you find out?" I asked.

"Could we just line them up?" Seth said. I nodded yes.

"See, I told you it would work," Abby said. They returned to work.

Maria and Timmy came to tell me the results of their circling 10s on Maria's dollar signs. "There are three 10s and 4 extras," Maria told me.

"And how many dollar signs altogether?" I asked.

"27," she said.

"That doesn't make sense to me," I said. "I think that three 10s make 30. I can count by 10s—10, 20, 30—and four extras would make 31, 32, 33, 34. So I don't know how you can get three 10s and four extras with 27 dollar signs."

Maria and Timmy were both confused. Maria's paper was hopelessly marked with circles around the dollar signs. "Take a marker of a different color," I suggested, "and circle 10s and see what you can find out."

I noticed that Gwyn and Sarah were drawing intricate patterns with colored markers. "Which activity are you working on?" I asked the girls.

"We were doing *0–99 Patterns,*" Sarah said, showing me her written work. "But now we're coloring."

"Yes, I can see that," I said, "but it's still math time. You're supposed to be working on the menu."

Sarah and Gwyn looked at each other. They are good friends and prone to socializing. "Choose an activity and return to work," I said. "I'll be back to check."

Maria came over to get me. "There are 26," she said. "I counted by 1s and 2s again and 10s. I got two 10s and there are six extras." I went to her desk with her to confirm her work. Timmy nodded his consent. At this time, neither Maria nor Timmy had any understanding about the relationship between the numerals and the 10s and 1s structure of our number system.

Nick and Rudy were still playing *Cover a Flat.* "He's winning," Nick said when I came by.

"By a lot or a little?" I asked. They both looked at their blocks.

"It looks like just a little," Rudy said.

"How much more does Rudy have?" I asked.

"What do you mean?" Nick asked.

"How much ahead of you is Rudy?" I asked.

"I don't know," Nick said.

Meanwhile, Rudy was examining the blocks. "I know," he said, "I've got one more rod and three more extras."

"Then you're one rod and three extras ahead," I said, "and that means you've got 13 more."

Rudy nodded. Nick looked confused. "Rudy, try and explain to Nick why that makes 13," I said.

I checked on Jonathan and Grace. They were playing *Race for $1.00* and were excited about what they had just discovered. "We have almost the same," Grace said, "but Jonathan has one more dime."

"How much do you each have?" I asked Jonathan.

"I have 51 cents and Grace has 41," he answered.

"Do you know how much more Jonathan has?" I asked them both.

"One more dime," Grace said.

"I have 10 cents more," Jonathan added. I've noticed that Jonathan is benefitting from his partnership with Grace. Grace is an animated child while Jonathan is more of a dreamer. Her energy seems to keep his attention from wandering.

Tomo came and got me again. "Come help," he said.

I went to their table. Colleen had rolled two 6s. "I told her just to take a dime and two pennies," he said.

"No," Colleen answered, "I want to do it this way." She showed me the 12 pennies she had counted.

"But it's so slow," Tomo complained.

"Is what Colleen did correct?" I asked Tomo.

He nodded and said, "But it takes too long that way and she keeps the pennies."

"I do not," Colleen said. "I've been trading them like Ms. Burns said."

They both looked at me. "As long as what someone does makes sense," I said, looking at Tomo, "then it's okay." Then I looked at Colleen. "But it's good to listen to your partner's ideas," I said, "and see if they give you another way to think about the game."

To shift their focus, I asked Colleen how much money she had altogether. "What do you mean?" she said.

"How much money is in your pile?" I asked again. She started to count the coins, sliding them over one by one, with no regard for the different value of dimes and pennies. I was beginning to understand Tomo's frustration.

I separated the dimes and pennies and showed her how I counted the dimes first and then the pennies. She had 53 cents.

"I'll do it again," I said, "and you count along with me." She did. Then I asked Tomo to count his money aloud while Colleen and I watched. He did so easily.

"After you each take a turn," I told them before leaving, "count the money and make sure you both agree." I was interested in seeing if Colleen's understanding or confidence increases. Colleen and Tomo's partnership is a challenge for them. They have widely different math abilities and social skills. I watch carefully to give them help.

I stood up and looked over the class. Sarah and Gwyn were now playing *Cover a Flat.* So were Corrine and Eli; they had switched from *Dollar Signs.* Maria and Timmy were talking with Nick. They had run into difficulty resetting the stopwatch they were using for *Dollar Signs* and had gone to Nick for help. I had appointed Nick the class stopwatch expert, and he was proud and patient. The six pairs who had started with *Race for $1.00* were still engaged with the game, Annie and Marina were still working on their papers for *Dollar Signs,* and Andrew was still working on *0–99 Patterns.*

Annie drew 46 dollar signs and counted them by 2s and 5s.

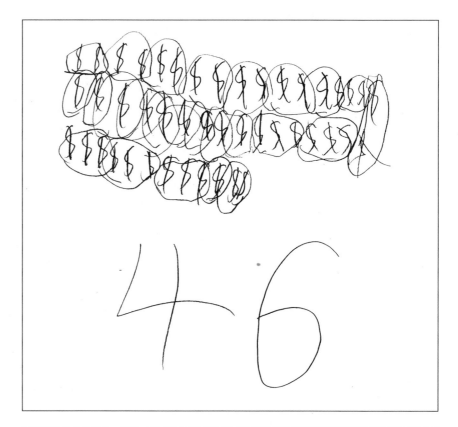

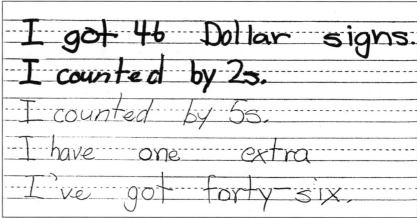

> I got 46 Dollar signs.
> I counted by 2s.
> I counted by 5s.
> I have one extra
> I've got forty-six.

When it was time to clean up, I reminded the children who had done written work to put it inside their folders. Also, I reminded them all to indicate the activities they had done with a check mark on their lists of the menu activities. After having one child from each table collect the folders and return them to the bin, I dismissed them for lunch.

The class had gone well. Actually, it was a dream day. The children generally worked well together. They were relaxed and engaged, and I had the opportunity to talk with a good number of them. Days like this in math class make my spirits soar.

Children's Thoughts about Math Time

Visitors come to our math class regularly, both teachers from nearby schools and students from education classes at the local universities. They usually have many questions about the unit in general and specifically about menu time.

About a week after introducing the menu activities, I asked the children to write letters about menu time. This was a good way to have them reflect on the class while also reinforcing the proper form for writing letters. We put the letters into a folder and presented it to visitors when they arrived.

In his letter, Teddy explained about the menu system. He wrote: *Dear Visitors, We get to choose wat we want to and it very fun and I like it a lot. And I like Race for 1 Dollar the most. And then wen we are done we put are papers in are follder. But we have I - P. We usually do -P- and that is all. from Teddy*

Grace included different information. She wrote: *Dear Visitors, We are having math menu. We had math menu 1. We are having math menu 2. We are only allowed to play some of them because we did not learn all of them. They are to much for us to remember all of them in once. We all have 1 folder. One side is for us to put papers that are not done yet. the other side is for us to put the done papers in. I means we do it ourselfs and P is for us to do with partners. love, Grace*

Some children explained a specific activity. For example, Rudy wrote: *Dear visitors, Math menu is very fun. My favorite game is Dollar signs. You get your very own follder and chek list. If you want here is how you play. First you get a stopwatch then you get 2 pices of plan paper then you time someone for 1 min. They draw doller signs and thats how you play. from Rudy*

Other children wrote primarily about their own experience. Jason, for example, wrote: *Dear Visitors, My name is Jason. My favoirte so far is Dollar signs and Race for $1.00. I have a folder and I did Race for $1.00 2 times and I did Dollar sgns 1 time. I means individual by your self and P means partner. from, Jason*

MENU ACTIVITY Race for $1.00

Overview

Pennies, dimes, and dollars offer a real-life application of our place value system. In this game, students roll dice to determine the number of pennies to take. When they have enough, they exchange pennies for dimes and dimes for $1.00. The goal is to get $1.00.

181

Race for $1.00

You need: Zip-top baggie with 30 pennies, 20
             dimes, and 2 play dollars
             2 dice

Rules:
1. Take turns. On your turn, roll the dice. The sum
   tells how many pennies to take.

2. Decide if you want to exchange.
   (10 pennies = 1 dime)

3. Give the dice to your partner.

4. Play until one player has $1.00.

Notes:
1. You may exchange only when you have the dice.

2. Watch to make sure you agree with your
   partner's moves.

From *Math By All Means: Place Value, Grade 2*   ©1994 Math Solutions Publications

---

Note: This activity, taught to a different class of children than described in this unit, appears on Part 2 of the videotape series *Mathematics: Teaching for Understanding*. (For information, see the Bibliography on page 193.)

Before the lesson

Gather these materials:

■ 1-quart zip-top baggies, each with 30 pennies, 20 dimes, and 2 play dollars (For play dollars, see Blackline Masters, page 192.)
■ Two dice per baggie
■ Blackline master of menu activity, page 181

Getting started

■ Show the class a baggie and describe its contents. Post the number of pennies, dimes, and dollars, and encourage children to check the contents of the baggie when they're finished playing.

■ Introduce the game by telling children that the goal is to get $1.00.

■ Explain to the class the rules on the menu task.

■ Be sure to emphasize the two notes at the bottom of the directions. Setting a procedure for when children can exchange and stressing the importance of children monitoring each other's moves helps them stay engaged talking about the game as they play.

■ After students are familiar with *Race for $1.00,* give them the homework assignment on pages 172–173.

■ After the children have had some experience with the game, read *The Go-Around Dollar* by Barbara Johnston Adams. (See Children's Books, page 168.) This book tells the story of the travels of a particular dollar bill while providing facts and anecdotes about dollar bills in general. After you've read the story aloud, leave the book out, so students who are interested can read it. At a later time, if a child finds a particular tidbit of information especially interesting, invite him or her to share it with the class. Also, children might be interested in writing their own stories about the adventures of a different dollar bill.

FROM THE CLASSROOM

Race for $1.00 was an easy game to teach and captured the children's interest because it used money. I colored in the box on the class chart next to the title of the activity and showed the class one of the baggies of money. "For this game," I said, "you need a partner, two dice, and a baggie of money."

"How much is in there?" Andrew said.

"I haven't figured it out," I said, "but I know there are 30 pennies, 20 dimes, and 2 play dollars." I wrote this information on the class chart next to the title of the activity.

"Can we figure it out?" Andrew persisted. For Andrew and several other children, figuring out the amount of money in the baggie would be an intriguing challenge. Others wouldn't be interested at all. Some children could figure it out without using the money, some would have to count the coins, and still others wouldn't be able to figure it out with or without money. This range in my class is, I think, typical of most second grade classes. I wanted to respond to Andrew's interest while also respecting the diversity in the class.

"Yes, it would be fine for you to figure it out," I said. "But please don't do that right now. I'd like to teach you how to play the game and also

introduce several other menu activities. When you get to work, you can choose to solve that problem first."

"Do we have to?" Timmy asked, nervous about this challenge.

"No, you don't have to figure out how much money there is in the baggie," I replied. "The menu activity is to play the game I'm going to teach you now."

I decided to model the game by playing with Maria. She was sitting at the front of the room, and we cleared her desk to play. Introducing an activity works better, I think, if I do it on the rug with the children seated in a circle. It's easier for them to see that way. However, I was introducing four activities and needed to use the chalkboard for one of them, so I had the children gather around Maria's desk as best they could.

"Would you like to go first?" I asked Maria.

"No," she said, "you go first."

I asked Teddy to read the directions aloud. "Just read the first rule," I said.

"Take turns," he began. "On your turn, roll the dice. The sum tells how many pennies to take." I rolled the dice, got a 5 and a 3, and took eight pennies.

"Now what?" I asked. "Please read the second rule."

"Decide if you want to exchange," he read. "Ten pennies equals one dime."

"I don't have enough pennies to exchange," I said. "Read the third and fourth rules."

"Give the dice to your partner," Teddy read. "Play until one player has $1.00."

I gave the dice to Maria and she rolled a 1 and a 3. She groaned and took four pennies. I waited a moment and asked her to give me the dice.

"Remember," I told the class, "don't just take the dice. Wait until the other person hands them to you. Also, you need to watch to be sure you agree with the number of pennies they take or if they exchange correctly."

Maria handed me the dice and I rolled them. This time I rolled a 4 and a 2.

"You get six," Eli said.

I took six pennies and then said, "I have enough to exchange ten pennies for a dime. Watch, Maria, to be sure you agree." I counted out ten pennies, returned them to the baggie, and took a dime. "So now I have one dime and four pennies; that's 14 cents." I handed the dice to Maria.

Maria rolled two 3s and took six pennies.

"How much do you have now?" I asked. Maria counted and found she had 10 pennies.

"You can exchange," Sarah told her.

"Do I have to?" Maria asked, looking at me.

"No, you don't have to exchange right now," I said, "but eventually you will have to in order to work toward getting $1.00. Would you like to exchange now or wait?"

"I'll wait," Maria said.

"Then pass the dice to me," I said. Maria gave me the dice.

"So that's how you play," I said. I decided not to continue with the game. The rules for the game are simple, and I thought that enough of the children had the idea to be able to play. I told them to return to their seats.

"Before I teach you another game, I want to read the two notes at the bottom of the directions," I said. "They're important for you to know." The two notes direct the children to exchange only when they have the dice

and to be sure to watch each other as they play.

"One more thing," I said. "It's a good idea to check your baggie before you return it to the supplies shelf to be sure you have the correct number of pennies and dimes."

I went on to introduce two other menu activities. Many of the students were excited about *Race for $1.00*. The attraction of money was a strong draw, and all the baggies were in use when the children went to work on the menu.

Linking assessment with instruction

When I circulate and supervise during menu time, I have several different kinds of questions I pose to children who are playing *Race for $1.00*. This activity is particularly useful for providing a vehicle to challenge children's thinking and help me assess their number sense. Sometimes I ask children how much money they would have altogether if they combined their coins. At other times, I ask them how much more they would need to get to exactly $1.00, or how much more one has than the other.

Assessing Seth and Abby

I interrupted Seth and Abby and asked them to tell me how much money they each had.

"I have 39 cents," Seth said. He knew how much he had without having to check. Abby, however, spread out her dimes and pennies to count. "I've got 46 cents," she said.

"If you put your money together," I said, "how much would you have?" I was interested in seeing how the children would solve this problem, specifically if they would think about regrouping pennies into a dime.

Seth and Abby slid their coins closer together, being careful not to mix their piles. Seth came up with an answer first. "It's 85 cents," he said. He had counted the dimes to get 70 cents, then slid one of Abby's pennies over a bit (still keeping their piles separate) to combine with his nine pennies for another 10 cents, and finally counted Abby's remaining five pennies. Abby, however, counted the dimes to get 70 cents and then proceeded to count the pennies by ones to finish. "I got 85 cents," she also said.

"And if you put your money together," I then asked, "how much more would you need to have in order to have exactly $1.00?"

"I've got to get a piece of paper," Abby said, while Seth started counting on his fingers. Abby's strategy was to write the number 85 and underline it. "That's so I know where I started," she said. Then she continued writing the numerals up to 100.

While she was doing this, Seth got an answer. "It's 15," he said, "we need 15 more cents."

"Let's see if Abby gets the same answer," I said. She had written all the numbers and was now counting them. Her concentration was impressive to me. "I got 15," she said. Both children seemed pleased. I left them to finish their game.

From this interaction, it seemed to me that Seth was more facile and confident with thinking numerically. Abby was more cautious, being careful and methodical both in her counting and in her writing. This is the sort of information that helps me form mathematical profiles of my students.

Two days later, Seth and Abby were playing the game again and I interrupted them. "You're going to ask us how much we have altogether, aren't you?" Seth asked.

"Yes," I said. "How much do you have?" Abby had 30 cents and Seth had 34 cents. It was easy for them to figure out that they had 64 cents altogether. They both counted the dimes and then added on the pennies.

"What question do you think I'll ask next?" I said.

"How much more we need to get $1.00," they both answered, more or less in unison.

"Try and figure it out," I said, "and then come get me when you've both agreed on an answer." I left them. They each decided to use paper and pencil to solve the problem. Also, both of them used the method Abby had used the last time, writing 64, underlining it, and then writing the numbers from 65 to 100. However, they got stuck when Abby got an answer of 36 cents and Seth got 33 cents. They were completely perplexed.

I looked at their papers and found Seth's error. "You left out some of the numbers in the 90s," I said. He corrected his error and then counted the numbers from 64 to 100, underlining each as he did so.

Seth wrote the numbers to figure out how much more money he needed to get from 63 cents to $1.00.

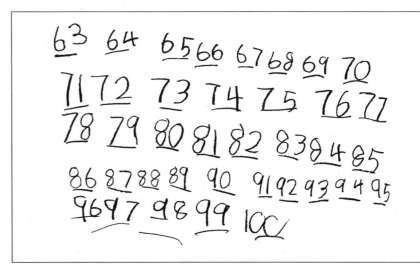

"How come you decided to use paper and pencil instead of counting like you did the other day?" I asked Seth.

"It was too far to count," he said. He paused for a moment and then added, "I think I should have counted."

"It's easy to make mistakes either way," I said. "I think it's a good idea to do a problem two ways to have a check, or to check with a partner as you did with Abby." I left them to continue their game.

Even though Seth made a careless error when he tried Abby's method, I saw his decision as willingness to be flexible about his approaches to problems. He had displayed this flexibility regularly since the beginning of the year. Abby's method seemed to make sense for this problem, and he tried it. Abby, on the other hand, was more limited in the approaches she was willing to use. When she had a method that made sense to her, she continued to rely on it and wasn't interested in other ideas.

Assessing Teddy and Katy

One day, I initiated a conversation with Teddy and Katy at the end of a game, just as Teddy had won. "I have a dollar and two cents," he said.

"How much do you have, Katy?" I asked.

"I have 95 cents," she answered. "It was close."

"Can you figure out how much more Teddy has?" I asked.

In a moment, Teddy blurted out an answer. "I have seven more."

"Do you agree?" I asked Katy. She shrugged.

"Can you explain to Katy how you figured it out?" I asked Teddy.

"I counted," he said. "I did 96, 97, 98, 99, 100, 101, 102." He kept track with his fingers. Katy seemed to understand.

"If you put your money together," I then asked, "would you have $2.00 or more than $2.00 or less than $2.00?"

"More," Teddy answered. "No, less."

"Less," Katy said.

"Take some time and figure it out," I said.

This time it was Katy who offered an explanation. "If I take Teddy's extra two cents, that gives me 97 cents," she said, "and that's not enough for an extra dollar."

Teddy was thinking while Katy answered. "We'd have a dollar and 97 cents," he said.

"That's what I said," Katy replied.

"So you both agree," I said. "What do you plan to do now? Play another game or switch activities?" I left them to discuss this.

Teddy was quick numerically and confident in his ability. When he was interested in a problem, he generally stuck with it and worked until he had an answer that satisfied him. He never seemed to get ruffled or be troubled when he made an error; he was curious and confident. Katy, on the other hand, was tentative about her math reasoning. She vacillated in her responses, sometimes being clear and other times confused, sometimes being willing and other times reticent. I felt she needed many more experiences to strengthen her understanding and build her confidence.

Assessing Molly and Amelia

When I interrupted Molly and Amelia, Molly had 37 cents and Amelia had 29 cents.

"How much do you have altogether?" I asked.

They looked at each other's coins and, like Seth and Abby, they were reluctant to intermingle them.

"Look," Amelia said, "if you put the pennies together, you'd have enough to trade for a dime."

"But how many extras would there be?" Molly asked. Amelia began counting on her fingers while Molly was focusing on the money.

"I think it's 16 cents," Amelia said.

"Wait a minute," Molly said. "I have to give you a penny and then you can get a dime and then I have six pennies left. So it's a dime and six extras."

"That's what I said," Amelia said.

"So how much do you have altogether," I asked, "counting all your dimes and pennies?"

"Oh, yeah," Molly said. They counted together and figured out the correct answer.

"I have one more question," I said. "How much ahead is Molly?"

"Oooooooh," Molly said, "that's hard."

"No, it isn't," Amelia said, and she counted on from 29 to 37, using her fingers. "It's 8."

"Do you agree?" I asked Molly.

"I'm not sure," she said. "Wait a minute, let me see."

"You just have to count," Amelia said.

Molly sighed. "Let's just play," she said.

This conversation confirmed my previous observations of Amelia and Molly. Amelia calculates mentally easily, more easily than Molly and many of the children in the class. Molly feels more comfortable when she relies on some concrete material or story context. Also, Molly is a bit of a dreamer and her attention tends to wander when she feels overwhelmed by a problem.

I left the girls to continue their game.

Catherine and Hassan's Not-Enough-Pennies Problem

One day, Catherine and Hassan ran into a problem with the money when they were playing *Race for $1.00*. The dimes and pennies in the bags had been redistributed, as children sometimes borrowed money from one baggie for another. On this day, Hassan had three dimes and seven pennies; Catherine had two dimes and nine pennies. There were plenty of dimes left in their supply, but only seven pennies. Catherine had rolled double sixes.

She came and got me. "What should I do?" she asked, almost wailing.

"What's the problem?" I said.

"I need to take 12 pennies and there aren't enough," she said.

"I told her what to do," Hassan interjected, "but she doesn't believe me."

"Can you tell me what Hassan's suggestion was?" I asked Catherine. She shook her head no.

"What was your idea?" I asked Hassan.

"I told her just to take a dime and two pennies," he said, "because that makes 12 cents."

"I don't get it," Catherine said.

"How much money are you supposed to take?" I asked.

"I got two 6s," she said, "and that's 12."

"Why do you think Hassan suggested taking a dime and two pennies?" I asked.

Catherine hesitated for a moment. Then she reached and took a dime and two pennies. She sat quietly for a moment and I just waited. Hassan was being very patient also, seeming somewhat intrigued with Catherine's pondering.

"Okay," she said in a musing tone, fingering the coins, "a dime is 10 cents and then you go 11, 12. . . . Oh," she said, looking up and brightening. "It works. It's 12 cents."

"That's what I told you," Hassan said in a somewhat superior tone.

"Yes, you made a good suggestion," I said. "But an idea only seems like

a good suggestion to someone else when it makes sense to them too." I left the children to continue with the game.

When Catherine gets confused, she's always quick to come to me for help, instead of stopping to think about the problem herself or seeking help from her partner or another classmate. Her number sense is weak, but her need seems as much emotional as mathematical. I was working to help her learn to rely more on herself and her partner.

Assessing Marina and Annie

I interrupted Marina and Annie one day and began the same way I did with the other students.

"Can you each tell me how much money you have?" I asked.

"I have 51 cents," Marina answered.

"47, no, 48 cents," Annie said.

"So who has more so far?" I asked.

"She does," Annie said. Marina nodded.

"How much more?" I asked.

Marina immediately started to think about the problem. She closed her eyes and brought one hand up to use her fingers. She counted softly to herself, "49, 50, 51." She did it again to check. Meanwhile, Annie screwed up her face. She seemed confused. She looked down at the coins and began rearranging them. She matched her dimes and Marina's dimes by arranging them into two columns and noticed that Marina had an extra dime.

"Is it 10 cents?" Annie asked hesitantly.

"No," Marina said, "it's only three cents. Look, you go 49, 50, 51." Marina use her fingers to illustrate her thinking.

"Oh, okay," Annie said.

I wasn't convinced Annie understood, as I knew her number sense was fairly weak. Marina, on the other hand, was confident about her math ability. She wasn't finished thinking about the money. "I think we have about $1.00 together," she said.

"How do you know that?" I asked.

Marina reached for a pencil and paper. She wrote *48¢* and *51¢* and underneath wrote *50 + 49 = 99*. "I put 1 from the 51 on the 48 so I have 50 and 49," she explained, "and that makes 99. All we need is one more penny."

Marina shows how she combined 48 cents and 51 cents.

48¢   51¢

50 + 49 = 99

Annie watched and didn't comment. I feel that conversations like this one give Annie models for thinking about numbers. I'm careful, however, to avoid having Annie feel that she's deficient by not emphasizing the need for getting a correct answer quickly and by not praising Marina for her math ability.

I left the girls to continue with their game.

MENU ACTIVITY

Overview

Dollar Signs

This activity asks children to do the same experiment they did in the whole class lesson *Stars in One Minute* (see page 41), but they draw dollar signs ($) instead of stars. Along with providing children with another opportunity to count a large number of objects in several ways, the activity also gives children experience with measuring time. Working in pairs, children take turns timing one minute for each other. After drawing the dollar signs, each child figures out in two different ways how many he or she drew and writes about the methods used to count.

182

Dollar Signs P

You need: A way to time one minute

1. One person times one minute, and the other person draws dollar signs ($).

2. Switch jobs.

3. After you've each drawn dollar signs, count how many you drew in two different ways.

4. Write about how you counted.

From *Math By All Means: Place Value, Grade 2*   ©1994 Math Solutions Publications

---

Note: This activity, taught to a different class than described in this unit, appears on Part 2 of the videotape series *Mathematics: Teaching for Understanding*. (For information, see the Bibliography on page 193.)

Before the lesson

Gather these materials:
■ Timers for timing one minute (if there isn't a class clock with a sweep second hand)
■ Blackline master of menu activity, page 182

Getting started

■ Remind the class about the whole class lesson, *Stars in One Minute*. Have several children recall how they did the experiment.

■ Review the directions on the menu task.

■ Explain carefully how the children are to record. You may want to write a prompt on the board to help children begin their writing.

■ Follow up this activity with the *Dollar Signs* homework assignment. (See Homework, pages 173–174.)

FROM THE CLASSROOM

I introduced *Dollar Signs* on the first day of the menu, right after I introduced *Race for $1.00*. Because we had spent a good deal of time on *Stars in One Minute*, I felt that the directions would be easy for the children to follow. I colored in the box in front of *Dollar Signs* and began my explanation.

"This is just like *Stars in One Minute*," I said, "but you draw dollar signs instead."

In the two previous years when I taught this unit, the classroom clock had a sweep second hand. This year, however, there wasn't one, so I had borrowed six stopwatches.

A few days earlier, I had taught Nick how to use the stopwatches—how to clear them and get them into stopwatch mode. I chose Nick because he's very good with machines of any kind. He's able to help others with the class computers, change the bag in the hand vacuum cleaner, fix the stapler, and make the pencil sharpener work. However, Nick also has difficulty staying focused during whole class lessons. He often gets excited, then a bit wild, and then loses his concentration. I felt that having some responsibility would be good for him and help him keep on track and stay engaged with the class. Nick was thrilled with the job and took the responsibility very seriously.

I showed the stopwatches to the class and showed them the button for starting and stopping the timer and the button for resetting the time. Several of the children were eager to investigate the timers.

"When you choose this activity," I said, "you'll be able to experiment with the stopwatches. Also, Nick knows how to reset them so they're back to zero. So, if you get stuck, ask him to help." Nick beamed.

I then asked Sarah to read the directions aloud: *One person times one minute, and the other person draws dollar signs. Then switch jobs. After you've each drawn dollar signs, count how many you drew in two different ways. Write about how you counted.*

I showed the children the two kinds of paper they needed to use, one for drawing the dollar signs and the other for recording.

"How do you know when a minute is up?" Timmy asked.

"You use one of the stopwatches," I answered.

"I know," Timmy persisted. "But how does it tell you?"

"Ah," I said, "we should talk about this. The stopwatch works like a counter. It counts by seconds, like some of you did when I had you close your eyes and estimate one minute. It takes 60 seconds to make a minute."

"I don't know how to do it," Timmy said. Timmy isn't very confident about his abilities and worries about not knowing.

"I can teach him," Nick said.

"Can I do it with Nick?" Timmy said.

"No," I answered. "You have to work with your regular partner. But you can both get help from Nick if you can't figure out how to use the stopwatch."

I then had the children get to work. The stopwatch was a big draw, but after six pairs had chosen the activity, the rest of the children had to make other choices. I find that the excitement with a new piece of equipment quiets down after children have had opportunities to satisfy their curiosity about it.

This task required very little supervision from me. Children understood the directions and were eager to do the activity.

As I observed over a period of days, I noticed that most students grouped by 2s and 5s. Nick, for example, wrote: *I counted by 2s and I had 30 then I counted by 5s and I still got 30.*

Tomo described how he counted by 2s and by 5s and got 23 both ways.

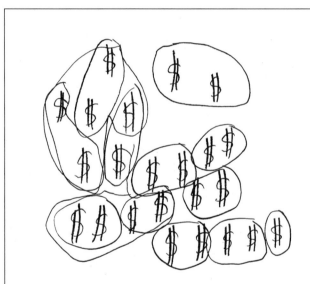

I counted by 2 ways 1 is 2 4 6 8 10 the 2nd way is 5 10 15 20 25 and when i counted 2 ways i got 23.

Leslie grouped her dollar signs by 2s and 1s.

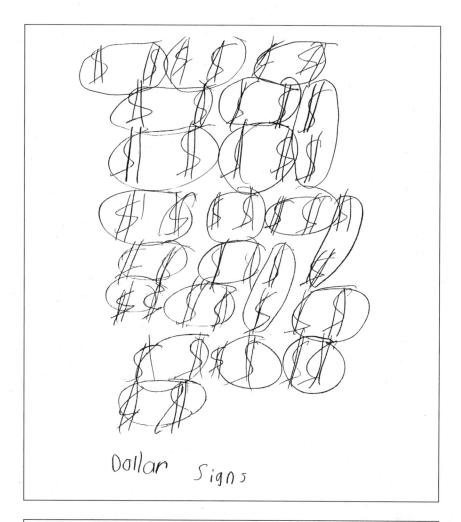

Dollar Signs

I couted By 2's and
I came up with 44.
I counted by 1's and
i came up with 44.

Some children counted by 1s. Leslie, for example, wrote: *I couted by 2's and I came up with 44. I counted by 1's and i came up with 44.*

Very few children grouped by 10s. In my experience, I've noticed that grouping by 10s isn't typically seen by children as useful for counting large numbers of objects. (If you were going to count a pile of objects, such as the raisins in a small snack box or the pennies in a jar, how would you group them?) Although grouping by 10s is useful when adding numbers, it isn't always useful in the context of working with concrete objects.

NOTE When teaching, choosing whether to impose procedures on children or to allow them to seek their own ways of making sense of situations is at the heart of professional decision making. When the goal of teaching is to help students construct understanding of mathematical ideas, it's more effective to give children the time and freedom to explore those ideas in their own ways. As a general rule, the students should push the curriculum, rather than the curriculum pushing the students.

Linking assessment with instruction

I used to insist on this task that children group by 10s. Actually, I included this direction on all activities in the menu. However, I've stopped doing so. I've come to realize that when I impose a system on children, they get invested in following my rules rather than understanding the sense in the procedure. I've seen many children who can circle groups of 10 objects and tell the total, but still not understand the 10s and 1s structure of our number system.

When I interacted with students during menu time, I often asked children who had counted their dollar signs to tell me how many groups they would have if they made groups with 10 in each. For Tomo, this was a simple question and he answered immediately.

"Three 10s," he said.

"Any extra dollar signs?" I asked.

He thought for a moment. "No," he said, with a tone of voice that implied that I had asked a stupid question.

"How do you know?" I asked.

"You just go 10, 20, 30," he said.

Leslie was able to identify that there would be four 10s and four extras if she grouped her 44 dollar signs into 10s.

"Convince me," I said.

"Okay," she said, "first you do the 40. That's 10, 20, 30, 40. Then you have to count the rest and you go 41, 42, 43, 44."

Jason, however, didn't have a clue about the number of 10s in his number. He had drawn 36 dollar signs. He counted them by 1s and by 5s. First he had gotten two different results, but after some recounting, he decided on 36.

"If you circled groups of 10," I asked Jason, "how many groups of 10 would you have?"

He thought for a moment. "Well," he said tentatively, "maybe one or two."

"Which do you think—one or two?" I asked.

"Hmmm, maybe two," he answered.

"Convince me," I said.

"I just guessed," he confessed.

"But what if you wanted to figure it out?" I replied. "What could you do?"

"I don't know," he said. "Oh, yeah, I could count and draw circles."

Maria had drawn 27 dollar signs. I asked her the same question I had asked the others, "If you circled groups of 10, how many groups of 10 would you have?" Maria didn't have a clue.

"Can I draw on my paper to figure it out?" she asked.

"Yes, but I wonder if you could try and figure out the answer first," I said. "How many circles would you have to draw if you counted by 10s?"

Maria sat quietly for a moment. Then she shrugged.

"Then try it on paper," I said gently.

Meeting a Special Need

When I assess students informally, I'm interested in gathering information that will help me form a picture of their mathematical interests and abilities. Generally, I don't use the information about students to alter my instructional program. The activities on the menu provide a variety of ways for students to interact with large quantities of objects and link them to the correct symbolization. Also, the menu activities are designed to be accessible to students with limited experience, while also being of interest to more confident students.

Sometimes, however, a student needs some extra attention. One day, Colleen called me over after she had counted her dollar signs. She had drawn circles to make groups of 2. "I got 28," she said, "but then I counted them by 1s and I got 34."

"Show me how you counted by 2s," I said.

Colleen began, but got confused in the teens, saying 15 after 14 and not sure what to say next. She started over, this time getting confused before she even reached 10. Colleen's number sense is very weak, and I sat down to talk with her. She didn't seem to have any understanding of even numbers. It seemed they were a string of words to be remembered, not a pattern of numbers to be understood.

"Show me how you would count the dollar signs by 1s," I said.

Colleen didn't have a system for keeping track of the dollar signs as she counted them. She missed one and counted two of them twice.

"How about counting once more," I said. "This time, put a tiny check mark next to each dollar sign that you count. That way, you won't miss any or count them more than once."

Colleen did this and got to 32. "But that's not the answer I got when I did it before," she said. She was confused and getting frustrated.

On my suggestion, Colleen used check marks to keep track of the dollar signs as she counted them by 1s. I used Xs to mark each group of 2.

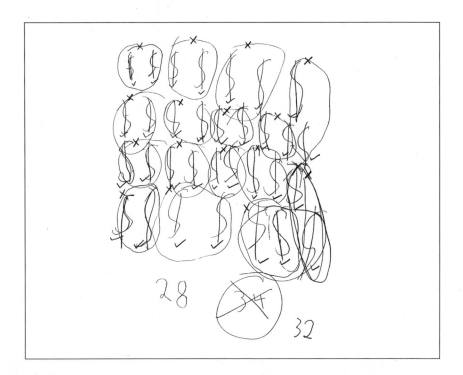

"That's why it's important to count several ways," I said, "just to check."

"Which is right?" she asked.

Getting the right answer to the number of her dollar signs seemed like the least of Colleen's problems, but it was important to her to know.

"Watch as I count by 2s," I said, "and we'll see what I get. I'll put a little *X* on each circle as I count that group." I counted by 2s and got 32.

"So it's 32?" she asked.

"Let's count again by 2s," I said. "This time, try and count along with me." Colleen was able to count with me up to 10, and then her voice faded.

"Would you like to know the secret of counting by 2s?" I asked her. She nodded yes.

"Would you be willing to do a special activity that isn't on the menu?" I asked her. She nodded yes again.

I had Colleen get the Snap Cubes. "Make a bunch of little trains with two in each," I said, "and then come and get me again."

"Does it matter what color I use?" she asked.

"No," I answered, "use any colors you'd like."

Colleen presented a special problem to me. Although she could count and used that as a way to add small quantities, she had little understanding of the relationships among numbers. I felt I needed to intervene. I was interested, however, in giving Colleen help without making her feel deficient. Responding to the needs of children like Colleen, Jason, and Maria while at the same time responding to the needs of children like Andrew, Leslie, and Tomo presents one of the big challenges of teaching.

Colleen called me over after she had made about a dozen trains of two. I moved the trains aside and put a piece of 9-by-12-inch construction paper in front of her.

"This is a game of count and record," I said. "You'll need a blank sheet of paper. How many cubes are on the construction paper now?"

"None," Colleen said, grinning.

"What number says none?" I asked.

"It's zero," she said. "Do you want me to write it?"

"Not just now," I said, "we'll get to that in a minute."

"Now I'll show you where the numbers come from when you count by twos," I said. "Just start by putting a train of two on the paper and then tell me how many cubes there are." Colleen did this easily.

"Put another train on and then tell me how many cubes there are altogether," I then said. Again, Colleen did this easily.

"So you started with zero," I reviewed, "then you had two, and then four." I removed the two trains from the paper, said "zero," and put each train back, counting "two, four" as I did so.

"Now add another train," I said, "and see how many cubes there were."

Colleen added a train and then counted the cubes by 1s, touching each cube as she counted. I cleared the paper again and counted by 2s from zero to six, putting the trains back on the paper. Then I had Colleen clear the paper and count by 2s as I had done, adding each train as she did so.

"How many do you think you'll have when you add another train?" I asked.

Colleen shrugged. "Oh, wait," she said, "it would be seven, eight. Eight."

"Try it and see," I said. Colleen added a train and again resorted to counting all the cubes by 1s. She was pleased to get to eight as she had predicted. I had her clear the paper and count by 2s to eight, adding trains

each time. I was trying to help Colleen link the sequence of even numbers to a concrete reference. I continued in the same way up until 12, and then told Colleen that I'd leave her to continue, but that I wanted her to keep track of the numbers so I could check later.

I cleared the paper again. "That's zero," Colleen said.

"Write the number for zero on your paper," I said.

"Anywhere?" she asked.

"Near the top," I answered, "so you have room to write others underneath."

Then I had Colleen add a train. "I've got two," she said. "Should I write that, too?"

"Yes," I replied, "write it under the zero." I showed Colleen how to continue listing the numbers and left her to work. She was interested and engaged. When she got to 20, she began to wonder about the numbers she had skipped and wrote them in a separate list.

Working with Snap Cubes, Colleen generated a list of even numbers, and then wrote a second list of the numbers she had skipped.

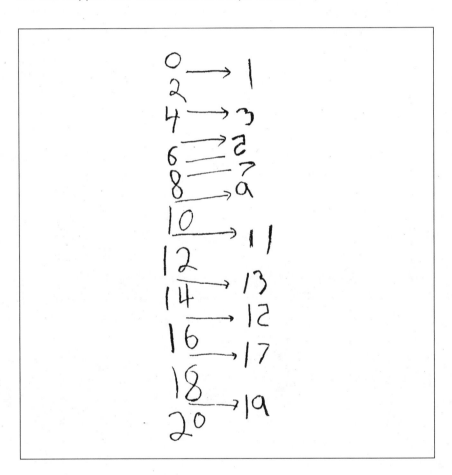

"Look," she said to me, "there's one in between all of them." She was surprised by this.

"Yes," I said, "those are the odd numbers." This information didn't seem to be of any interest to Colleen, another reminder that children learn on their own timetables. Later, I would have her color in the numbers on her list on a 0–99 chart and see the patterns that emerged. Children often benefit from several different ways to think about an idea.

NOTE There are children in every class who would benefit from extra teaching time and different approaches to help them make sense of mathematical ideas. It's difficult to find time to work with individual children in the midst of the general class bustle. It's also difficult to know the exact sort of help that would be most effective. However, it's important to make time for students in need and search for ways to offer extra assistance.

I wasn't interested primarily in "fixing" Colleen's lack of understanding of even numbers. This lack was merely a symptom of the holes and confusions in her mathematical understanding. Although the activity focused specifically on the pattern of even numbers, I was interested in having Colleen see that number patterns come from logical, orderly relationships and in giving her an experience that could help reveal the logic and order to her. For many children, mathematical ideas are a jumble of random and isolated notions. They don't expect to see the order or logic and therefore don't even look for it. I was trying to influence Colleen's basic understanding of mathematics while, at the same time, giving her access to the rationale for the pattern of even numbers.

Although I never have a surefire way to effect a student's learning, I know that it helps enormously to give children personalized attention, have them link abstractions to some concrete reference, and help them see the connection between standard numerical symbolism and a concrete experience.

MENU ACTIVITY

Cover a Flat

Overview

Cover a Flat is essentially the same as *Race for $1.00* but uses Base Ten Blocks instead of money. It also offers a spatial model for thinking about place value that is particularly helpful for some children. The point of the game is to completely cover a hundreds square with tens rods. Children take turns rolling dice to find out how many unit cubes they can take, and they get tens rods by trading 10 cubes for each. The game provides children concrete experience with regrouping.

183

Cover a Flat

You need: 2 flats, 20 tens rods, 30 unit cubes, and a pair of dice

Rules:
1. Each takes one flat.

2. Take turns. On your turn, roll the dice. The sum tells how many unit cubes to take. Place them on your flat.

3. Decide if you want to exchange 10 unit cubes for a tens rod.

4. Give the dice to your partner.

5. Play until one player covers his or her flat.

Notes:
1. You may exchange only when you have the dice.

2. Watch to make sure you agree with your partner's moves.

From *Math By All Means: Place Value, Grade 2* ©1994 Math Solutions Publications

---

Before the lesson

Gather these materials:
■ Blackline master of menu activity, page 183
■ Zip-top baggies, each with 30 unit cubes, 20 tens rods, and two hundreds squares
■ Two dice per baggie

Getting started

■ Show the class a baggie and describe its contents. You may want to list the number of cubes and rods and encourage the children to check the contents when they're finished playing. (Note: If the children have not had experience with these materials, be sure to provide time for free exploration.)

■ Ask children how many unit cubes are needed to cover one flat. (With children, I use "flat" and "hundreds square" interchangeably.) Have all those who offer answers explain their reasoning. It most likely won't be obvious to all children that the flat has 100 squares, but don't worry about this; children can still play and learn from their experience with the game.

■ Introduce the game by telling the students that the goal is to cover the hundreds square.

■ Explain to the class the rules on the menu task.

■ After students have had experience with this activity, see *Assessment: How Much Is Covered?* on page 116.

FROM THE CLASSROOM

To introduce *Cover a Flat*, I began by coloring in the box on the large chart. When I began to explain the directions, Gwyn raised her hand and told me that they had played this game in first grade.

"That's good," I said, "then you already know how to play." I don't worry when children have experienced an activity previously. They enjoy repeating activities that interest them, and they bring the benefit of their past experience.

"The idea of the game," I said to the class, "is to completely cover the flat with ten orange rods." I showed the children a baggie in which I had put 2 flats, 20 tens rods, and about 30 unit cubes.

"Can I read the rules?" Gwyn asked. Because she remembered the game, she seemed to feel some ownership.

"Yes, you can," I answered, "but first I want to ask the class a question." I held up a hundreds square and one unit cube and asked them how many cubes they thought would fit on the square.

Andrew knew immediately. "It's 100," he said.

"How do you know?" I asked.

"Because there's 10 in a row," he said, "and 10 rows and that makes 100." Andrew is an extraordinary boy who announced to me one day that he was a "big number kind of kid." I've come to believe him.

"Any other ideas?" I said.

"You could count by 10s," Amelia said. "Can I show?" I nodded, and Amelia came to the front of the room and counted by 10s, running her finger down each row as she did so.

"Does anyone have a different way to figure?" I asked. There weren't any more volunteers. I wasn't convinced that all children knew that 100 unit cubes would cover the flat, but I decided that they would have a chance to figure it out when they were playing the game and were close enough to a hundreds square to get their hands on it.

I then chose Jonathan and Eli to play the game at a table in front of the room and had Gwyn come up to read the rules. I posted an enlarged version for the class to follow.

"Read the rules step-by-step," I said, "so that Jonathan and Eli can follow them."

Gwyn began with the materials. "You need 2 flats, 20 tens rods, 30 unit cubes, and a pair of dice," she read. I gave the boys the baggie of blocks and a pair of dice.

"Rule one," she continued, "Each takes one flat. Rule two: Take turns."

She stopped at that point and said to the boys, "You have to decide who goes first." Jonathan and Eli looked at each other. Neither of them is particularly competitive, and after a few moments, Eli said that he would go first. Jonathan nodded his agreement.

Gwyn continued to read, "On your turn, roll the dice. The sum tells how many unit cubes to take. Place them on your flat. Three: Decide if you want to exchange 10 unit cubes for a tens rod. Four: Give the dice to your partner."

Eli rolled the dice. A 4 and a 5 came up and he counted the dots. "It's 9," he said.

"Do you agree, Jonathan?" I asked. Jonathan hadn't done the addition and looked over at the dice.

"Yes," he said, "you go 5, then 6, 7, 8, 9." He used his fingers when he counted.

"So what are you going to do, Eli?" I asked.

"Take nine cubes, Eli," Sarah said.

"I know," Eli said. He took nine unit cubes and lined them up on one row of the hundreds square.

"You can't exchange," Gwyn said, "because you don't have enough, so you have to give the dice to Jonathan."

"That's an important rule," I reinforced. "Your partner can't just take the dice. You have to hand the dice over to your partner when you're done with your turn."

Eli gave Jonathan the dice and he rolled them. He got a 2 and a 1. "That's only 3," he complained, and put three unit cubes on his flat.

"Now give Eli the dice," Gwyn instructed.

Eli rolled them, this time getting two 3s. "It's 6," he said quickly. The doubles are always easy for the children to remember.

"Do you agree, Jonathan?" I said, to reinforce that partners were supposed to pay attention to what each other was doing. Jonathan nodded. Eli added six unit cubes to his flat.

"You can exchange," Gwyn said.

"I know," Eli retorted, a bit annoyed that he was being rushed. He carefully counted 10 unit cubes, not making use of the information that there were 10 in one row of the hundreds square. He replaced them with a tens rod.

"Now give the dice to Jonathan," Gwyn directed.

"Wait a minute, Eli," I interrupted. "First, tell the class what you have on your flat right now."

"I've got a rod and five little ones," he said.

"Do you know how many little squares on your flat are covered up by the tens rod and the five unit cubes?" I asked.

"It's 15," he said.

"Raise your hand if you agree that Eli's blocks cover 15 squares," I said to the class. More than half of the children raised their hands.

"Who can tell how they know?" I asked.

I called on Seth. "It's 10 and 5 more and that's 15," he said.

Leslie had another idea. She counted on from 10. "You can go 10 and then 11, 12, 13, 14, 15," she said.

No other children had suggestions, so I asked Eli to pass the dice to Jonathan.

Jonathan rolled a 3 and a 4. He counted on his fingers and got seven. Eli was figuring in his head and the boys said "7" at the same time. Jonathan reached for the unit cubes.

"You'll have just enough to exchange for a tens rod," Andrew said. Jonathan ignored him, however, and counted out seven unit cubes and placed them on his hundreds square. Then he counted all the unit cubes, found he had 10, removed them, and put one tens rod in their place.

I thought that this was sufficient to introduce the children to the game. I thanked Gwyn for helping with the directions. I reminded children about exchanging only when they had the dice and watching each other as they took their turns. Then I told the children to discuss with their partners which activity they'd like to choose. Also, I told Eli and Jonathan that they could continue their game or choose another. They decided to finish the game and Eli rolled the dice.

Linking assessment with instruction

As I circulated, I interacted with those who were playing *Cover the Flat* similarly to the way I interacted with children who were playing *Race for $1.00*. I was looking for opportunities to assess individual children's understandings and would ask different questions, depending on what I already knew about the children and where they were in the game.

For example, sometimes I'd ask them if they had enough blocks to cover a flat if they combined all the blocks each of them had. I posed this question to Nick and Hassan one day when they were almost halfway through a game. Nick had five tens rods and three unit cubes on his flat; Hassan had four tens rods and eight unit cubes on his.

"I don't think so," Nick said.

"How do you know?" I asked.

"I just guessed," he said.

"How could you figure it out?" I asked.

"There are almost enough tens rods," Hassan said. While Nick and I were talking, he had counted their tens rods. "There's nine," he continued. "I think we'll have enough."

Nick got interested. "Oh, yeah," he said, "maybe we can get another rod." He began counting their unit cubes.

"It works!" Hassan was pleased. "We'd have one more extra little one."

"How many squares have you covered so far on your flat, Nick?" I asked.

"53," he said.

"And you?" I asked Hassan.

"48," he answered.

"So 53 plus 48 is a whole flat plus one extra. How much is that?" I asked.

"What do you mean?" Nick asked.

"I know," Hassan said. "There's a hundred on the flat, and then one more, so it's 101."

"Oh, yeah," Nick said.

"So 53 plus 48 is 101," I said. "Do you think you'd get that answer if you pressed *53 + 48* on the calculator?" I am always looking for ways that children can use calculators to confirm their thinking. Also, I wanted to help the boys see the connection between our number system and the game.

Each boy reached for a calculator and tried it. They are still clumsy with calculators and often push buttons incorrectly. Nick got 101 and Hassan's display showed 5348.

"Try it again," I said to Hassan, "and be sure to press the plus sign."

"Here, I'll show you," Nick said, reaching to grab Hassan's calculator. Hassan held his calculator out of Nick's reach.

"No," he said, "I want to do it." Nick cleared his own calculator and did the problem again. This time, both boys got 101. They returned to their game.

Sometimes I asked children to tell how many squares they each had covered and compare the amounts, figuring out how many more squares one had covered than the other. This sort of problem wasn't too difficult when the game was close and both had the same number of tens rods. It was easy to compare visually. (If done numerically, no regrouping would be needed.) For example, when I interrupted Molly and Amelia, Molly had three tens rods and two cubes, while Amelia had three tens rods and seven cubes. It was easy for the girls to see that Amelia was ahead by five cubes.

However, when I interrupted Teddy and Catherine, they weren't able to arrive at an answer. Teddy had 27 squares covered and Catherine had 34.

"Teddy has more little ones," Catherine said, "but I have another rod."

"I could get another rod," Teddy said.

"But then you'd be ahead," Catherine answered.

I made a suggestion. "Suppose you got some more unit cubes, Teddy, so you could exchange for a tens rod, and still have four left over to match Catherine."

Teddy and Catherine looked at their flats and were silent. After a moment, Teddy became animated. "I know," he said, "I could roll a 10 and get a rod, and Catherine could roll a 3 and get more cubes. Then we'd match." So much for my suggestion.

Sometimes I phrased the question differently and asked children to figure how many more blocks the person with fewer would need so both of them would have the same number of squares covered on their flats. Usually I did this because making a numerical comparison seemed too difficult for the children.

For example, I interrupted Leslie and Jason one day. "Who has covered more squares so far?" I asked. They looked at each other's flats and agreed that Jason had more. He had two tens rods and three unit cubes; Leslie had one rod and seven cubes.

"How many more?" I asked.

"That's hard," Jason said.

"Do you know how many squares you've covered?" I asked.

"I've got 23," he said.

"And I covered 17," Leslie said.

"So how many more would have to be put on Leslie's flat so it matched Jason's?" I asked.

"I need to put on one more rod and take off some cubes," she said. "I'd have to take off four little blocks."

I nodded and left the children to continue with their game. I'm always surprised when children have a different way of thinking about a situation than I do. Leslie made sense of the situation in a way that hadn't occurred to me but seemed logical. Her response was a reminder to me not to hold a preconceived notion of what I'd like a child's response to be, but to be curious about what they might say.

I probed with another question. "What do you need to roll, Leslie, so you'd get the blocks you need to match Jason?"

She was stumped. Her answer of putting on one more tens rod and taking off four cubes didn't help her with my question.

"Oooh, look," Jason said, "if you got a 6 it would work. Then, you'd be up to me." He was looking at their hundreds squares and suddenly had seen a new way to think about the problem.

I squelched my thought about probing further as I felt Leslie and Jason's attention drifting. I was eager for the children to connect their concrete experience to numerical reasoning, but I knew this wasn't the right time. I left the children to continue their game.

NOTE When questioning children, it's important not to have a set notion about how they "should" reply, but instead to be open to their responses and listen intently. The focus should be on children's expressions of their thinking and reasoning processes, not on their giving correct answers.

ASSESSMENT How Much Is Covered?

It's not necessary for all assessments to be done individually. Having children work in pairs on an assignment provides the additional opportunity to listen to their conversations while they talk about the problem they're solving.

This assessment draws on children's experience with the menu activity *Cover a Flat*. (See page 110.) The problem is:

> Two children were playing *Cover a Flat*. One had covered 28 squares on her hundreds square; the other had covered 35 squares. If they put all of their blocks together on one flat, how many squares would they cover?

You may either write the entire problem on the board and have children read it to themselves or have a volunteer read it aloud. Or tell the problem and record just part of it:

> One child covered 28 squares.
> One child covered 35 squares.

Also, before having children solve the problem, you might want to have a brief class discussion about whether or not the children have enough blocks to cover entirely one flat. This discussion can help focus students on the problem.

Give children directions for working on the problem:

1. First, they tell each other the problem and make sure they both understand it.

2. Then they talk about how they could solve it.

3. Finally, they solve the problem and explain their thinking on paper. If they each have different methods, they should write about both of them.

FROM THE CLASSROOM

This problem came from an actual situation when Molly and Amelia were playing *Cover a Flat*. Although the assessment relates to an activity introduced early on in the unit, I waited until later to assign it, after I had information about children's individual approaches to addition. Also, I wanted to be sure that all of the children had experience with the game and, therefore, would be comfortable with the context of the problem.

For this assessment, I had children work in pairs. I decided to change the partners they had been working with on the unit and explained my reasoning to the class.

"I have a problem for you to solve that's about *Cover a Flat*," I said. "You'll do this with partners, but for today, you'll work with someone other than your usual partner."

"Can we pick our own partners?" Sarah said.

"No," I answered, "I picked partners for today, and let me tell you why. I've been noticing the different ways you've been solving some of the problems I've been giving you, and I've put together children who have been using different methods. That way, I think you'll have the chance to learn about another way to think about numbers."

I then reseated children so they were next to their new partners. I told them that when they were finished, they could continue working with the new partner for the rest of the period, but they would return to their regular partner the next day.

Next, I introduced the problem. "I interrupted Molly and Amelia a few days ago when they were playing *Cover a Flat*. Molly had covered 28 squares and Amelia had covered 35 squares." I wrote on the board:

Molly covered 28 squares.
Amelia covered 35 squares.

"I asked the girls if they had enough blocks to cover entirely one flat if they combined them," I continued. "What do you think? Talk about this for a minute with your new partner."

I gave the children a moment to talk. I was interested to see which children would estimate to answer my question, if any would add to get an exact answer, and who would be stymied. After a few minutes, I called the class back to attention and began the discussion by called on Leslie.

"I don't think they have enough," she said.

"Why not?" I asked.

"It's just doesn't seem possible," she explained, "because Molly would only have two rods and Amelia would have three, and that's not enough to cover it all."

Several other hands were raised. "Does anyone have a different idea?" I asked. I called on Katy.

"My idea is like Leslie's," she said. "It isn't different."

"Let's see if there are any different ideas," I said, and called on Eli. He had a calculator in his hand.

"It's not enough," he said. "You don't get to 100." Several other children reached for calculators to test Eli's idea. There are calculators for the children in the supply basket on each table.

Andrew was waving his hand wildly, and I called on him next. "It's easy," he said, "you need 50 and 50 to make 100, and they both have less, so it's not enough." Andrew's response is a typical indication of his number sense.

Some of the children with calculators were agreeing with Eli. Others were perplexed by the information their calculators were providing them. At this time in the year, almost half of the children still weren't comfortable with calculators and didn't see them as useful problem-solving tools.

I called the children back to attention and asked them to return the calculators to their baskets. I then told the children the problem I wanted them to solve.

"Eli used the calculator to figure out how many squares Molly and Amelia's blocks would cover. That's the problem you have to solve with your new partner," I said.

"Can we use the calculator?" Nick asked.

"You can," I said, "but you also have to figure it out without the calculator so I can learn more about how you think about numbers. Listen to my directions so you understand what you're to do." I waited until I felt I had everyone's attention.

"First, you are to tell each other the problem to make sure you both understand it," I said. "Then, you need to talk together about how you might solve it. Third, solve the problem and explain your thinking on paper. If you each have different methods, you need to write about both of them."

I wrote abbreviated versions of the directions on the board and reviewed them with the class:

1. Tell.
2. Talk.
3. Write.

"Who can explain what the first direction means, what you have to 'tell' each other?" I asked. I waited and only about half of the children raised their hands.

"I notice that only about half of you have your hands raised," I commented. "I'm going to have someone explain. Be sure to listen. Then I'll ask again who understands what the first direction means."

I repeated my question. "Who can explain what you have to 'tell' each other?" I called on Gwyn.

"You have to tell the problem so you both understand it," she said. I nodded.

"Raise your hand if you think you know what this direction means," I said, pointing to number 1 on the board. All but five children raised their hands.

"Some children still aren't sure," I said, "so who else can explain the first direction?" I called on Seth. "Listen carefully," I said, calling a few children's names to get their attention.

"You tell the story so you're sure you both know it," Seth said.

"Raise your hand if you think you know what this direction means," I repeated, again pointing to number 1 on the board. All of the children raised their hands. I take this time with directions to make sure that the children know I think that listening to directions is important. I have two dreamy children, and several who have difficulty paying attention, and this sort of focus is especially helpful for them, while useful for everyone in general.

I continued in the same way for the next two directions.

"Are there any other questions?" I asked before having them get to work.

Annie raised her hand. "Can we get blocks to use?" she asked.

"Yes," I said, "as long as you follow the three directions."

"Can we do it with the calculator?" Jason asked.

"Yes," I said, "but you also have to figure it out without the calculator and explain as the directions say."

There were no other questions. I gave each pair of children a sheet of paper and they went to work.

Seven pairs of children divided their papers, and each child wrote separate solutions. On Nick and Abby's paper, for example, Nick wrote: *35 Add 10 45 Add 10 55 Add 8 63.* Abby, however, resorted to her usual method of counting on by writing numbers. She wrote 35, underlined it, and then wrote 28 more numbers: *35 36 37 38 39 40 41 42 43 44 45 46 47 48 49 50 51 52 53 54 55 56 57 58 59 60 61 62 63 Yes.* She circled 63.

Nick and Abby showed their different ways of solving the problem.

"Do you understand each other's methods?" I asked them.

"I understand hers," Nick said. "She just counted."

"I kind of get his," Abby said, "but not really."

Jonathan and Gwyn also divided their work and didn't seem to communicate with each other. Jonathan used his usual method of drawing tallies and counting, grouping by 5s; it's unclear how he got 63. Gwyn explained two ways, by drawing a hundreds square and coloring in 63 squares and also by writing: *I thingk its 63 becuas if you take 20 and 30 = 50 + 10 = 60 + 3 = 63.* She also wrote: *20 + 30 = 50 + 5 + 8 = 63.*

Gwyn explained how she solved the problem numerically and also made a drawing to illustrate her solution. Jonathan, however, used tally marks and didn't indicate how they helped him arrive at the answer.

On their paper, Tomo used the standard algorithm, as he usually does. Eli wrote: *20 + 30 = 50 and if 8 + 5 = 13 and if you add them togethr it will be 63.*

I was pleased to see that Marina made use of 10s and 1s. Her paper indicated that she no longer was reverting to the faulty rule she had been using. (See pages 38–40.) She wrote: *I added the 10's and then added the 1's and I got 63.* Her partner Leslie wrote: *So you got 35 + 20 = 55 + 8 = 63.* "Our ways are almost the same," Leslie told me.

Marina and Leslie both used 10s and 1s but expressed their reasoning in different ways. They also figured out how many more were needed to cover entirely one flat.

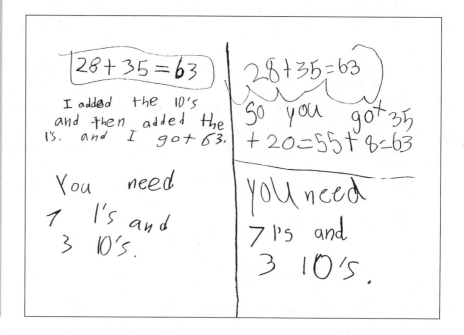

Some children gave just one answer. Seth and Rudy, for example, wrote: *10 + 10 + 10 + 10 + 10 = 50 + 8 = 58 + 5 = 63. Both Seth and Rudy.*

Molly and Katy started by using the same method Abby used, writing 35 and then writing the numbers afterward to count on. They wrote: *We didnt like this. and switched to use tally marks.*

Annie and Catherine worked together, adding the 10s and then counting the rest on their fingers. They wrote: *We just figurd it out. We had 50 and we cownted the left overs. And we got 63.*

MENU ACTIVITY

0–99 Patterns

Overview

This activity extends children's experience from Part 2 of the whole class lesson *The 0–99 Chart.* (See page 23.) Students examine one another's patterns, guess the rules they used, and check their theories in an answer booklet. The activity provides children the opportunity to continue their investigation of the organization of numbers on the 0–99 chart.

184

0–99 Patterns $\boxed{\text{I}}$

You need: 0–99 patterns

1. Choose a 0–99 pattern, figure out the rule, and write it.

2. Check your answer. If you disagree, talk with the person who made the rule.

3. Do this for at least 5 patterns.

P.S. If you'd like, make other puzzles, put them in your folder, and I'll add them to the class supply.

From *Math By All Means: Place Value, Grade 2* ©1994 Math Solutions Publications

Before the lesson

Gather these materials:
■ The 0–99 chart patterns the children completed during Part 2 of the lesson *The 0–99 Chart.* (See page 23.) Number the top and bottom of each child's chart pattern with the same number and cut each paper in half. Staple all the 0–99 charts into one booklet and all the descriptions of their patterns into another. Put a construction paper cover on each, labeling one "0–99 Patterns" and the other "Answers to 0–99 Patterns."
■ Blackline master of menu activity, page 184

Getting started

■ Choose one of the student's patterns to model the activity for the class. Show the class the 0–99 chart and have them give you suggestions for what the rule might be.

■ Record what you think the rule is on the board.

■ Show the class the student's rule and ask them to compare it with what you've written on the board.

■ Explain to the children that they are to do the same sort of investigation for one another's patterns. Read the directions on the menu task.

■ Point out to the class that the activity is an individual activity and that if they work together, they still must each record individually.

FROM THE CLASSROOM

This menu activity asks children to examine the patterns on other students' 0–99 charts, figure out the rules, and then check their theories in the answer key. I colored in the box in front of *0–99 Patterns* on the class chart of menu activities and showed the children the materials I had prepared.

"In this activity," I explained, "you get to look at one another's charts and figure out the patterns."

"Is it partner or individual?" Sarah asked. She is a social child who prefers to work with a partner.

"It's an individual task," I answered. "It's okay to discuss your thinking with your partner, but you each have to do your own writing." This was not new information for the children, as we had been using the system since the beginning of the school year. However, I've found it's necessary to reinforce the procedure from time to time, and Sarah's question provided a natural opportunity to do so.

I returned to introducing the activity. "Here's Leslie's 0–99 chart pattern," I said, "the one she showed us during our whole class lesson." I chose Leslie's pattern because we had discussed it. I held up her chart to help children recall that she had colored in 3, 12, 21, and 30.

"If I were doing this menu activity," I continued, "I'd have to guess Leslie's rule and write it on a sheet of paper." To model how to record, I drew a rectangle on the board to represent a sheet of paper and wrote my name, the date, and the title: *0–99 Patterns.* I also wrote the number *1* since that was the number of Leslie's pattern.

"Let's see," I said, thinking out loud. "I think that Leslie's rule is that she colored in just four numbers." I wrote on the board:

The pattern is to color in just four numbers.

"That's not right," Teddy commented, remembering Leslie's pattern from the class discussion.

"Next, I need to check my idea," I said, ignoring Teddy's remark. I located Leslie's pattern in the answer key.

Leslie and some of the other children were shaking their heads no. "That's not it," Leslie said.

"No, it's not it," I said. "Leslie's description says: 'All the ones that equal three.'"

"You have to add," Leslie reminded me.

"Since Leslie's description is different from what I wrote," I said, "I need to go to Leslie and have her explain her idea. Can you explain it to me, Leslie?"

"See," she said, "1 and 2 makes 3, and 2 and 1 makes 3, like that. They all make 3."

"Do you have to change what you wrote?" Nick asked.

Much of teaching demands that we make decisions on the spot. I hadn't considered Nick's question ahead of time and responded with my initial thought. "That's not necessary," I said, "because your idea may not be wrong. It may be just a different way to describe the same pattern of numbers. You can change your sentence if you'd like, but it's okay for you to leave it." Although my answer seemed satisfactory to Nick, I wasn't sure if it was the best response.

"Let me try another pattern," I said. "I don't have to do them in order, so I can pick any one I want." As I talked, I rummaged through the pile and removed another pattern. "Here, I'll try number 10." This was Gwyn's pattern and all of the numbers in the 70s row were colored in as well as the numbers in the column that ended with 7. The number 7, however, wasn't colored.

"Does anyone have an idea?" I asked. About half the class raised their hands and I called on Jason.

"They all have a 7 in them," he said.

"Yes, that seems to be true," I said. I wrote the number 10 on my "paper" on the board and recorded what Jason said. "But how come she didn't color in the number 7?" I asked. "There must be something else."

I called on Amelia next. "They're only the numbers that have two digits," she said.

"That's it," Hassan said.

I added Amelia's idea. I now had written:

They all have a 7 in them and they are numbers with two digits.

"Any other ideas?" I asked. No other children raised their hands.

"Now I have to check the answer key," I said. I found Gwyn's description and read it to the class. She had written: *Thay have two digits and thay all have #7 in them.*

"We both agree," I said, "so I don't have to check with Gwyn."

NOTE So much of teaching requires that we think on our feet and make decisions in the moment. It's easier for teachers to respond to new and unexpected questions when teaching a lesson with which they are familiar. When doing something for the first time, however, teachers often don't have the depth of experience to make on-the-spot decisions. Just as children's understanding of and comfort with math ideas grow and deepen with experience, so do teachers' understanding and comfort with math lessons grow from experience.

"How many do we do?" Seth asked.

"That's a good question," I said. "Let's read the task and see what the directions say."

I read the directions to the class. I then asked, "Who can answer Seth's question about how many patterns you should investigate?"

I called on Molly. "You have to do at least five," she said, "but you can do more."

"That's right," I said, nodding. "Now there's one more part to the directions. It's a 'P.S.' on the bottom that says: *If you'd like, make other puzzles. Put them in your folder and I'll add them to the class supply.*"

The introduction to this activity took a bit longer than I had intended, but I think it was worth taking the time to make sure the directions were as clear as possible.

This activity seemed to provide an intellectual refuge for children who felt the need for time to work by themselves on a quiet activity. When they chose the activity, children didn't need any help and were, therefore, self-sufficient.

Linking assessment with instruction

As I circulated around the class during menu time, I observed that children responded in three different ways to the activity. Some did the activity as I had intended—choosing a pattern, deciding what the rule might be, recording it, and then checking it. For example, after looking at Andrew's pattern, Amelia wrote: *I was right. I solved andrew's 0–99 pattern's. It is all the number's that have nine's in them from 0–99. There are 19 numbers inclouding 9 itelfe. The shape of the pattern's Look Like a L. It is fun.*

Amelia had quite a bit to say about Andrew's pattern.

> I Was right I solved
> andrew's 0-99 pattern's IT IS
> all the number's that have
> nine's in them from 0-99 There
> are 19 numbers inclouding 9
> itelfe. The shape of the
> pattern's Look Like a L
> It is fun

Amelia's paper had spelling and punctuation errors, and she had mis-used apostrophes consistently, an error I've found to be common when children first learn about them. Also, she had underlined the words that she wasn't sure about spelling, as the children have been instructed to do in all their writing. However, I didn't talk with her about these errors. I don't have children edit all of their work. For menu activities, I'm more interested in their thinking about the mathematics than focusing on a product. Their menu recordings are not typically shared publicly, and I think of them as the children's records of their mathematical tinkering.

Amelia's paper, however, sparked my thinking, and I mentioned this to her. I told her that her comment that there were 19 numbers in the pattern interested me. "I hadn't thought about investigating how many numbers fit the rules," I said. "Your paper started me wondering about rules that would use lots of numbers, 50 or more." I try and give children feedback about my reaction to the content of their work rather than my judgment of it. As much as possible, I want to keep the emphasis of our interaction on thinking about mathematics.

Some children responded differently to this task and didn't provide the detail that Amelia did. Gwyn, for example, wrote that she had looked at patterns from Abby, Andrew, Jonathan, and Molly. She wrote a sentence for each. For example: *All of the numbers with 7.*

Gwyn recorded the rules for the patterns she chose.

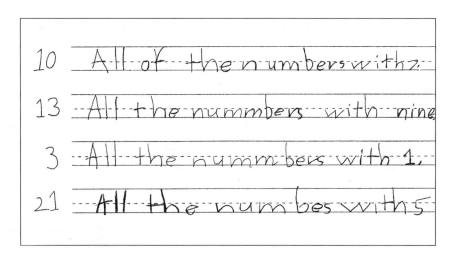

When I looked at Eli's work, I noticed that his recording didn't provide any information about his thinking about the patterns. For each pattern he investigated, he wrote a similar sentence: *I solved Molly's paterne on 11-18-92.* When I stopped to chat with him, he showed me his work proudly.

"I've done five already," he said, showing me the two sheets on which he had recorded. Each paper had his name, the date, and the name of the activity. For Eli, this was a big improvement over his previous work, and I wanted to acknowledge his attention to the mechanics and also talk with him about my need to understand his thinking.

"Your papers are very clear," I said. "They've got your name, the date, the name of the activity, and the name of the person whose pattern you looked at." Eli beamed. "Were the patterns easy for you or hard?" I asked.

Eli wrote that he solved the others' patterns, but he didn't provide any information about the rules.

I solved Andrew's Paterne on 11-18-92

I solved Molly's Paterne on 11-18-92

I solved Leslie's paterne on 11-18-92

0-99-patterns. 0-99 Patterns. 0-99 gatterns.

"Kind of both," he said.

"Give me an example," I said.

"Sometimes it's easy to guess and sometimes I can't get it," he said.

"Let's look at Molly's pattern," I said, choosing it because it was on Eli's desk. "What did you notice about it?"

"It's all the numbers with 5s," Eli said.

"Oh, I see," I said. His description was correct. I also questioned him about Andrew's pattern.

"I'm glad we talked, Eli," I said, "because talking helped me learn about how you were thinking. You didn't write about any of your ideas on your paper."

"Do I have to go back and do it all over?" he asked.

"No," I said, "but know that it's important for me to understand how you're thinking, and it helps when you give more information."

Eli nodded. I know that writing is hard for him, and I wanted to be gentle. Eli returned to work, choosing Leslie's pattern. He continued several days later, examining Nick's, Amelia's, and Catherine's patterns. He continued his same form of recording, and I made the decision not to demand anything more from him at this time.

Some children got involved producing additional patterns. I created new booklets for their patterns and rules. When I added a few new patterns, I called them to the class's attention. This usually sparked a renewed interest in the task, or at least a reminder for children who hadn't as yet chosen it.

NOTE While it's ideal for all children to engage fully with each activity, it rarely happens. It's important to strive for presenting mathematical activities that involve children with limited experience and ability as well as intrigue and challenge those with more experience and ability. The art and craft of teaching demands that we decide how to acknowledge children's efforts, when to accept their work, and how and when to challenge them to go further. Responding to children during menu time calls for being understanding, compassionate, encouraging, and more.

There was a good deal of variety in students' patterns.

0–99 Chart

They have two digits and thay all have #7 in them.

0–99 Chart

my patern is a diagonal and all of the diagonal equals up to 9

0–99 Chart

My pattern is all eights at the end.

MENU ACTIVITY

Overview

Number Puzzle

Number Puzzle extends students' experience from the whole class lesson *The 0–99 Chart.* (See page 22.) Each child writes the numbers from zero to 99 on a blank 10-by-10 grid, glues the chart onto tagboard, and cuts the chart apart into 7–12 puzzle pieces. Students then try to piece together one another's puzzles. Both making a puzzle and solving others' puzzles helps deepen children's familiarity with the orderliness of the numbers on the 0–99 chart.

185

Number Puzzle

You need: a 0–99 number puzzle

1. Put the puzzle together to make a 0–99 chart.

2. Sign your name on the back of the envelope to show you solved it.

3. Put the pieces back into the envelope.

4. Do at least 5 people's puzzles.

From *Math By All Means: Place Value, Grade 2* ©1994 Math Solutions Publications

---

Before the lesson

Gather these materials:
■ Blank 10-by-10 grids, one per child, plus five or six extras (See Blackline Masters section, page 186.)
■ Blackline master of menu activity, page 185
■ One 10-by-10 grid on which you've written the numbers from 0 to 83
■ 9-by-12-inch tagboard, one sheet per child, plus several extras
■ Letter-size envelopes, one per child, plus several extras
■ A shoe box to hold the envelopes
■ Glue
■ Scissors

Getting started

■ Show the children the grid on which you've written the numbers 0–83. As they watch, complete the numbering to 99.

■ Glue your 0–99 chart onto tagboard, spreading the glue all over the sheet so that pieces will stay glued when you cut them apart. As you glue, explain to the children that they'll each fill in a chart as you did to make a puzzle for others to solve. Point out that they must have you check the numbers on their charts before gluing them to tagboard and that they must spread the glue because they will be cutting their charts apart and want the pieces to stay together.

■ While the glue is drying, explain to the children that after the glue dries, you'll cut the chart into 7 to 12 puzzle pieces and put the pieces into an envelope. Show the envelopes and the shoe box you'll use to hold the envelopes.

■ When the glue has dried, cut your chart into 7 to 12 pieces. Point out that students must cut only on the lines.

■ Write your name or initials on the back of each puzzle piece. Tell the children this is so pieces can be identified if they get misplaced. As students watch, write your name on an envelope and place your puzzle pieces inside. Also, write on the envelope the total number of puzzle pieces. Put the envelope in the shoe box.

■ Tell the children that they'll each make a puzzle in the same way, and that, as a menu activity, they'll have the chance to solve one another's puzzles. When they solve one, they are to write their name on the envelope, put the pieces back inside, and return the envelope to the box.

■ After students have had some experience with the *Number Puzzles*, give them the homework assignment on page 174.

FROM THE CLASSROOM

I began the lesson by showing the class my partially filled grid. I had them watch as I wrote numbers from 84 to 99 in the remaining squares. Several of the children counted along as I wrote. Then I glued my chart onto tagboard, spreading the glue well.

I talked with the class while I waited for the glue to dry. "You'll each make a puzzle the same way that I'm showing you," I said. "First you'll write the numbers from 0 to 99 on a blank grid. Then you'll show it to me

so I can check it. Once I've checked it, you'll glue it onto a piece of tag as I just did. I spread the glue well so that the chart and the tagboard will stay together after I cut my puzzle pieces."

I showed the class the shoe box. "We'll keep all of your puzzles in this box," I continued. "Then, as a menu activity, you'll have the chance to solve other people's puzzles."

The glue seemed dry enough by then. First, I cut along the outline of the grid. "Now, I have to cut my grid apart into puzzle pieces," I explained. "The rule is that you have to cut on the lines, and you should wind up with no fewer than 7 pieces and no more than 12 pieces."

"Oh, I get it," Jason said. "Then we get to put it back together."

"That's right," I said. "Watch as I cut. I'm going to try and make some interesting shapes. And I'm going to try and cut my grid into ten pieces."

As the students watched, I cut my grid into pieces of various sizes and shapes. After cutting three pieces, I asked, "If I want to have ten pieces altogether, how many more do I need to cut?" Several children murmured answers and some raised their hands. I waited a moment to see if others would raise their hands. Finally, I called on Katy.

"You need to cut seven," she said.

"How do you know?" I asked, continuing with my cutting.

"I can tell on my fingers," she said.

"Does anyone have a different way of figuring?" I asked.

Nick raised his hand. "You go 3, then 4, 5, 6, 7, 8, 9, 10," he said, raising fingers as he counted from 4 to 10. "There are seven," he concluded.

Hassan raised his hand. "It's easy," he said, "because 7 plus 3 is 10."

By this time I had cut another piece. I continued cutting until I had six pieces. "How many more do I still need?" I asked. Again, I had children who were willing to volunteer tell the answer and explain their thinking. Questions such as these were trivial for some children, within reach for others to figure out, and too difficult for some. In any case, when I ask children for answers, I always ask them to explain their reasoning. Not only do their explanations provide me with insights into students' thinking but explaining helps children cement or extend their thinking and also introduces others in the class to ideas that might not have occurred to them.

When I had 10 pieces, the last piece was fairly large. "I think I'll cut this apart and make a few more pieces," I said. I did so and wound up with 12 puzzle pieces.

"You'll keep your puzzle pieces in an envelope like this one," I said, showing them the envelopes I had. "But pieces can fall out, so you should write your name on the back of each piece." As I was writing my name on the back of my pieces, a few children raised questions.

"Can we just put our initials on the backs of the pieces?" Molly asked.

"That would be fine," I replied.

Amelia raised her hand. "But Andrew and I have the same initials," she said.

"You can use your middle initials, too," Hassan said. That sparked a discussion about who had middle names and what they were. After a moment I called them back to attention.

"Any other questions?" I asked.

Seth raised his hand. "Can we write the numbers starting with 1 so we'll get to 100?" he asked.

I thought for a moment. "That's fine with me," I said. The question took me by surprise, but I couldn't think of a reason why it wasn't an okay idea.

"Can we write them in a different order?" Eli asked.

Again, the question took me by surprise and I thought for a moment. "No," I said, "not for this puzzle. I want to be sure that the numbers give clues to putting the puzzle pieces together, so they need to be in an order we're all familiar with. But that's a good idea for trickier puzzles, and maybe we'll do some of those later on." Eli seemed satisfied with my answer.

"Are there any other questions?" I asked.

Grace had one. "Do we write in pen or pencil?" she said.

"I suggest that you use pencil," I answered. "That way, if you make a mistake, you can erase and correct it."

"Can we used colored markers?" Gwyn asked.

"If you'd like, you can write over the pencil with a marker after I've checked your chart," I answered.

There weren't any other questions, and I gave one final direction. "When you have your puzzle made," I said, "then take an envelope, put your name on it, and put the pieces inside."

The children got to work. Practically all of them worked diligently and with concentration. It was interesting for me to watch children's systems for filling in the numbers. All but three of the children wrote the numbers in consecutive order, some counting out loud from time to time to check.

Jonathan, however, worked around the edges of the chart. He showed me his half-finished chart. "It's funner to do this way," he said and returned to work.

Gwyn had filled in the top row and the left-hand column. "This is so I can keep a check," she told me. She then did the rest consecutively.

Andrew started the same way as Gwyn had. But then he kept filling in numbers from the top and left, working across the chart toward the lower right.

"Something's wrong on my chart," Teddy said. He had filled in the entire grid and wound up with 98 instead of 99 in the last space. I found two 67s and helped him erase the numbers after that. He sat down to finish.

As the children finished, they brought their charts to me. Once I checked them, the children glued them to tag. I reminded them to wait for the glue to dry before cutting.

By the end of class, about half the children had completed their puzzles and were trying someone else's or working on a different menu activity. The rest of the students finished their puzzles the next day.

Linking assessment with instruction

For some children, solving number puzzles was easy because they were familiar with the pattern of numbers on the 0–99 chart. When I asked Seth how he went about putting together a puzzle, he said, "I look for all the beginning numbers."

"Which numbers are those?" I asked him.

"Like 10, 20, 30, 40," he said, "those numbers."

Molly used a different strategy. "I just find numbers that go in order and try and line them up," she said.

Annie did it another way. "The chart helps me." Annie was sitting near where the large class 0–99 chart was posted, and she referred to it for clues.

Other children, Maria and Colleen, for example, struggled to get the pieces to fit together. What seemed obvious about the pattern of numbers to children like Seth and Molly didn't occur to them. And even when they got help from someone else, they resorted to their own cruder method of trial and error when left on their own.

MENU ACTIVITY

Fill the Cube

Overview

While giving students further experience with counting large numbers of objects, *Fill the Cube* is a measurement activity that involves the children with estimating. Also, by comparing the number of popcorn kernels and lentils that fill the cube, students are challenged to reason proportionally.

187

Fill the Cube   I

You need: 1 Unifix cube with tape on the bottom
1 baggie of popcorn
1 baggie of lentils

1. Estimate: How many kernels of popcorn do you think will fill the cube? Record.

2. Fill the cube with popcorn. Then count the popcorn at least two different ways. Record and explain how you counted.

3. Repeat: Now do it with lentils. Estimate, Count, Record.

4. Write: How did your two counts compare?

From *Math By All Means: Place Value, Grade 2*   ©1994 Math Solutions Publications

---

Before the lesson

Gather these materials:
■ Blackline master of menu activity, page 187
■ Six 1-quart zip-top baggies, half-filled with popcorn
■ Six 1-quart zip-top baggies, half-filled with lentils
■ 12 Unifix cubes, each with a piece of masking tape over the small hole on one end, one in each baggie
(Note: These materials are sufficient for six pairs of students to do the activity at the same time.)

Getting started

■ Show the class the materials you've prepared. Explain that you've taped the small hole on the Unifix cube so that the popcorn or lentils won't fall through.

■ Begin by asking the students to estimate the number of kernels of popcorn they think will fill a Unifix cube. Model for them how to record their estimate by writing on the board:

I think there are ___ kernels of popcorn in the cube.

■ Do not count to verify their estimates; leave that for them to discover when they do the activity. However, tell them they are to count the popcorn in two ways and record. Write on the board:

I counted by ___ and by ___.

■ Pose the following question: *Suppose there were 50 kernels of popcorn in the cube. How many lentils do you think there might be?* You may want to distribute the baggies of popcorn and lentils so children can more easily compare their sizes. Have children offer their ideas and explanations.

■ Show the class how to record their estimates and counts for the lentils.

■ Review the directions by reading the menu task.

■ After students have experienced this activity, see *Assessment: Catherine's Problem* on page 140.

FROM THE CLASSROOM

To introduce *Fill the Cube,* I asked for a volunteer to read the directions. I chose Nick and posted a poster-size copy of the activity so the other children could follow along. I told Nick that he was to stop after each part so that I could demonstrate for the children what to do.

Nick began reading: *You need 1 Unifix cube with masking tape on the bottom, 1 baggie of popcorn, and 1 baggie of lentils.*

I showed the children the materials I had gathered. I had prepared 12 small plastic zip-top baggies, 6 with popcorn, 6 with lentils, and each with a Unifix cube. I had put a piece of masking tape on the bottom of each cube so that the popcorn and lentils wouldn't fall through.

Nick continued reading: *1. Estimate: How many kernels of popcorn do you think will fill the cube? Record.* I helped Nick pronounce "estimate" and "kernels." Then I asked children for estimates. Their guesses ranged from about 20 to about 100. I didn't offer an estimate because I didn't want to influence their thinking, but instead focused on modeling for them how to record. I drew a rectangle on the board to represent a piece of paper, wrote my name and the date in the upper right-hand corner, titled the paper "Fill the Cube," and then wrote:

1. I think there are ___ kernels of popcorn in the cube.

"I haven't thought yet about an estimate," I said, "so I didn't fill that in. But you should put down your guess when you record."

"Do we have to write just like that?" Catherine asked.

"No," I said. "What's important is that you put your name, the date, the title on your paper. Then you can use any words you want as long as your sentence explains that you're estimating popcorn and tells how much your estimate is."

"Could you start with like 'My estimate is' instead of 'I think'?" Teddy asked.

"Yes," I said, "as long as you include what you're estimating and how much your estimate is."

I then asked Nick to read the next direction. He read: *2. Fill the cube with popcorn. Then count the popcorn at least two different ways. Record and explain how you counted.*

"That's the same as *Dollar Signs*," Leslie said, "because you have to count in different ways."

"I think there are other activities on the menu that match," Andrew said.

"What do you mean?" I asked.

"Well," he said, "*Dollar Signs* goes with *Fill the Cube* and *Race for a Dollar* is the same as *Cover a Flat* and *0–99 Patterns* is like *Number Puzzle*."

"Actually," I responded, "I think all the activities are alike in some way."

"Yeah, well, they all have to do with math," he said.

"That's true," I said, "but they also all have to do with making sense of large numbers of things."

As Andrew and I were having this conversation, I filled a cube with popcorn kernels. "You'll need to spill the popcorn onto your desk. Then count them by 2s, 5s, 10s, or any other way that you'd like. And then record." I added to my "paper" on the board:

2. I counted by ___ and by ___.

I asked Nick to keep reading. He read: *3. Repeat: Now do it with lentils.* He was unfamiliar with the "lentils" and stumbled over the word. I showed the children a baggie of the lentils. Some children were familiar with lentils and others weren't. So they could examine them more closely, I distributed a baggie of lentils and popcorn to each table, asking the children not to open the baggies at this time. We talked for a few moments about lentil

NOTE One of the benefits of the menu is that it engages children not only with mathematics but with reading and writing as well. It's helpful to reinforce for students that the written directions contain all the necessary information for the tasks. Referring to the directions when introducing a task helps to remind children to refer to them when they need information or clarification.

soup. Hassan, whose father is from Iran, was the class expert. Grace, a Korean girl who had been living in the United States for only a year and a half, had never heard of them. Nor had several other children. Some thought they might have. Although a discussion about lentils and soup is certainly a digression from the activity, I thought it was important to spend a brief amount of time honoring their questions and knowledge.

"I have a thinking question," I said, returning to the mathematics. "Suppose I filled the cube with popcorn and found there were 50 kernels. How many lentils do you estimate would fill the cube?"

Several hands shot up. I called on Sarah.

"I think it would be 60," she said.

"Why do you think that?" I asked.

"It seems that the lentils are smaller than the popcorn," she said, "so more would fit."

I called on Hassan next. "I think 100," he said, "no, maybe a little less, like 95." Hassan seemed to come alive in a new way from the recognition for knowing about lentils.

"Why do you think that?" I asked.

"Because I think if you hold a lentil up to the popcorn," Hassan explained, "it looks like it would take about two of them to make a popcorn. Well, not exactly two, but a little more, so I think it wouldn't be exactly 100, but it would be 95."

I was surprised by this explanation. It seemed very sophisticated for a second grader.

Rudy had another thought. "It depends on how you hold the lentil," he said. "If you hold it sideways, then maybe two or three would match the popcorn, but if you hold it up and down, then it would be different."

"So how many lentils do you think will fill the cube?" I asked.

"I don't know," he answered, "maybe just 50 or maybe 100."

"Well, you'll have a chance to test your predictions if you choose this activity," I said.

The children were eager to get to work on the menu. I gave them my usual directions. "Talk with your partner about the activity you'd like to do today," I said. "When you and your partner have decided, raise your hands. After you've told me, one of you should go and get the materials you need."

Linking assessment with instruction

Although most of the students were initially interested, their reactions differed once they got involved with the activity. While some children enjoyed counting the popcorn and lentils, for example, others thought it was tedious to figure out how many of each there were. While some children used the information from their popcorn count to estimate the number of lentils that would fill the cube, others didn't attempt to draw any relationship between the two. While some children were upset when their estimates didn't agree with their counts, others just accepted the differences. I've come to expect different reactions and take time for students to express what they like and don't like about an activity. I've found that airing their likes and dislikes can serve to dispel children's concerns and helps them refocus on the task.

Some children seemed eager to write about their results. For example, Annie wrote: *I gusts [guessed] 31 and it was 32. I counted by 10's. I counted the lentils and I gusts 51 and it was 57.*

Annie, Amelia, and Katy's papers show the variety of student writing in the class.

> fill the cube
>
> I gusts 31 and it was 32. I counted by 10's. I counted the lentils and i gusts 51 and it was 57.

> fill The cube.
> I Thingk there is 14 popcorns. But there is 33. I guess I Was Wrong. I thingk there is 75 and I Was right. There is 75 of them inside of a cube.

> Fill the cube
> Think 33. anste 32.
> Think 53. anste 80.   2 46

Hassan wrote: *My guess is 38. It was 31. I cotid by 1. There wer 7 more. Then my estimate for my lentils is 61. the lentils was 46. It was 15.* Hassan was proud of the extra figuring he had done.

Amelia wrote: *I thingk there is 14 popcorn's. But there is 33. I guess I was wrong. I thingk there is 75 and I was right. There is 75 of them inside of a cube.*

Other students, however, struggled to get even a few words recorded. Katy, for example, wrote: *Think 33. ansre 32. Think 53. ansre 80.*

Catherine ran into a snag. She started with the lentils and guessed that it would take 49 to fill the cube. She filled the cube, spilled the lentils carefully on her desk, and counted to make a pile of 49. There were still more lentils, however. Catherine counted them separately, found there were 17 more, and wrote: *I gesst 49. It was 17 more.* Then she came to me for help.

"Come see," she said, taking my hand to lead me to her desk. I saw the two piles and read her paper.

"So far, so good," I said.

"But I don't know how to figure how many there are altogether," she said.

"I told her to just count them," said her partner, Hassan.

"There's too many," she said, whining. "I'll mess up."

"That's why I think it helps to put them into groups," I said. "Can you count by 10s?"

Catherine responded by counting by 10s to 100.

"How about putting the lentils into groups of 10 and then counting by 10s?" I suggested.

A while later, she brought her paper to me. She had added: *There is 66 all togethr. I got 66.* I decided to use Catherine's problem on another day for a class assessment. (See page 140 for a description of this assessment.)

ASSESSMENT Catherine's Problem

FROM THE CLASSROOM

Catherine's menu work from *Fill the Cube* was the catalyst for this assessment.

Catherine's Problem is similar to the *Numbers on the 0–99 Chart* assessment as it also presents children with an addition problem that requires regrouping. In this problem, the children are to add 49 and 17. Giving addition problems at different times is valuable for getting information from students to compare with previous assessments.

This problem came from a situation that occurred during menu time when Catherine was working on *Fill the Cube*. (See the *Fill the Cube* menu activity, page 134.) She was stumped by the problem of figuring out the total number of lentils she had in two piles, one with 49 lentils and the other with 17. The next day, I took the opportunity to present the problem to the class. I had children solve it individually so that I could use their papers to assess the class in general and individual students as well.

Clearly, this same situation will not occur in your classroom. Another might arise that suggests an addition problem to present to your students. However, if not, consider telling your class the story about Catherine's problem and asking them to solve it. As long as they've had experience with *Fill the Cube*, Catherine's experience will be familiar to them.

I explained to the class the situation that Catherine had faced on Friday when she was working on *Fill the Cube*. "Catherine had estimated that there were 49 lentils in the cube," I said. "Then she began to count them. She got to 49 and still there were more. So she left the 49 lentils in one pile and counted the rest. There were 17 in the second pile."

"That's when I got stuck," Catherine said.

"Yes," I said, "Catherine was having trouble figuring out how much 49 and 17 were altogether."

"I did it though," she said.

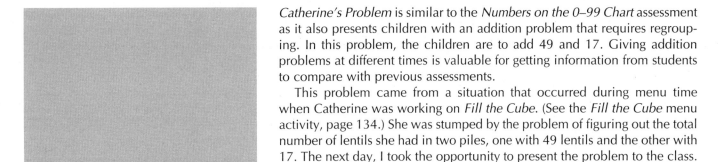

Fill The Cube
(1.) I guess 23. Popcorn
I counted By 1s
It was 29
There was 6 more Than I Thouthe
I counted 2 piles of 10 and I counted 9
extra.

(2.) I gesst 49
It was 17 more
There is 66 all together.

"Catherine was able to solve the problem," I confirmed. "What I'm interested in now is seeing how the rest of you would solve this problem. If you counted 49 lentils, and then counted 17 more, how many would you have altogether?" I wrote the problem on the board:

Catherine's Lentils
Catherine counted 49 lentils, and then counted 17 more. How many did she have altogether?

I gave further directions as I distributed paper. "Be sure to describe your thinking with numbers and words and, if you wish, pictures as well. When you've finished, and I've accepted your paper, then choose something from the menu to do."

"What should I do?" Catherine asked.

"Try the problem again," I answered, "and see if you can figure out a different way to solve it."

As I circulated throughout the class, I encouraged children to explain their thinking as fully as possible. I noticed a good deal of improvement since the beginning of the year in their willingness and ability to solve and write about a problem, but the students still needed prodding.

I analyzed the class set of papers later. Ten of the children solved the problem correctly using some method of regrouping. For example, Teddy wrote: *You take 40 from the 49 and 10 from the 17 and you have 50— and then you ad 7 and 9 and it macs 66.*

Rudy wrote: *I came up with 66 becaus 49 + 17 = 66 so just add 10 to 49 and you get 59 add 7 get 66.*

Molly had a solution that was unique in the class. She wrote it numerically: $49 + 17 = 50 + 16 = 50 + 10 = 60 + 6 = 66$. Because the representation of her thinking was clear to me, I did not require her to write more.

Teddy used 10s and 1s to do the adding.

> Catherine's Lentils
> you take 40 fohom the 49 And 10 from the 17 And you HAve 50— And then you AD 7 and 9 And it MAcs 66 ←

Even though Molly didn't use words, I accepted her paper because the numbers communicated her thinking clearly.

Catherine drew 17 tally marks and counted.

Leslie chose to use interlocking cubes, although she generally is comfortable working with numbers. She wrote: *I used snap cubes. I counted by 10's and I got 66.*

Grace did the problem correctly with the standard algorithm, as she usually does, but she still couldn't relate what she was doing to 10s and 1s. Grace doesn't yet have any real understanding about what "carrying" means. I've tried relating her calculations to pennies and dimes and to the Base Ten Blocks, but she hasn't made the connection yet.

Ten of the children got the correct answer by some method other than thinking about 10s and 1s. Four drew tally marks or circles; three counted on, writing the sequence of numbers; three wrote that they had used their fingers.

One of these children was Catherine. She didn't use the lentils or any other material. Instead, she drew tally marks and wrote: *I strtid with 49 and I droo 17 tale mrcs and I canted 66.*

Eli shows a mix of using 10s and 1s and counting on.

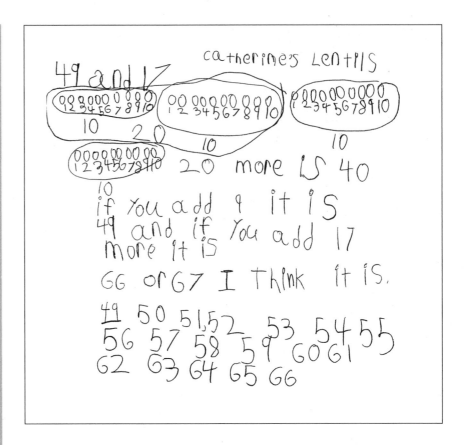

Eli's method was a mix of using 10s and 1s and counting on. He showed on his paper that he knew that 49 was four 10s and nine 1s, but he treated 17 as 17 1s. This didn't surprise me, as I've noticed other children apply the 10s and 1s structure to the numbers 20 and larger while not making use of the structure for the numbers in the teens. This may be because the language pattern of the numbers in the teens does not support the use of grouping by tens. If the numbers 10, 11, 12, 13, 14, etc. were read as "ten," "tenzy one," "tenzy two," "tenzy three," "tenzy four," etc., then the structure of 10s and 1s might become obvious to children more easily or sooner. However, we have to live with the language we have and help children broaden their understanding to see the link between the structure and the ill-named numbers.

I talked with Sarah about her paper. She had written the problem numerically, then did something to the numbers that made no sense to me and got the correct answer of 66. I've seen Sarah do this sort of thing before, seeming to try and bully numbers into submission. She wasn't able to give any reason for what she did. I told Sarah that her calculation didn't make sense to me even though her answer was correct. She sighed and said, "Okay, I'll do it another way." She resorted to counting on and came up with the correct answer. As a socially aware child, Sarah had noticed others solving similar problems by working with the numbers. She seemed to be trying to figure out a way to do something with the numbers as the others did, but it seemed that her social awareness surpassed her numerical ability. She hadn't yet found a way that made sense, either to her or to me.

Marina made a terrific breakthrough.

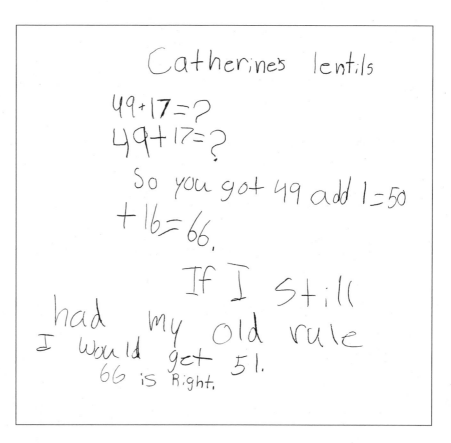

Catherine's lentils

49 + 17 = ?

49 + 17 = ?

So you got 49 add 1 = 50 + 16 = 66.

If I still had my old rule I would get 51. 66 is Right.

Five of the children found no way to tackle the problem. These children were uncomfortable with numbers larger than 10. Four of them recorded the correct answer, but they'd gotten it from a neighbor and couldn't offer any reason, either in their writing or when I talked with them.

The big breakthrough of the day was with Marina. She gave up the faulty rule she had been consistently using to add—for today at least! (Her method was to add the 10s and record, then add the 1s, recording only the 1s digit of that answer. See pages 38–40 in the *Numbers on the 0–99 Chart* assessment for a description of how Marina used this method to add 26 and 17 to get 31.) To solve Catherine's lentil problem, she wrote: *49 + 17 = ? So you got 49 add 1 = 50 + 16 = 66. If I still had my old rule I would get 51. 66 is right.* This change of mind made worthwhile all the effort I've made to help Marina see that her method made no sense.

From Assessment Back to Instruction

I often have children show their papers and present their methods to the class. However, I decided to try a variation on this method, one that I thought would promote more interaction among the children. I decided to pair the students, each with a partner who had used a different method for solving the problem, and have them spend part of a math period explaining their solutions to each other. My prediction was that this experience would be most helpful for Seth, Hassan, Sarah, Leslie, and Grace, the students who are most social and communicative.

Seth counted on, the method he trusts most for adding.

I tried this a few days after the assessment. I presented the plan to the class by first talking with the children about the importance of making sense of what they do in math. I told them I was going to return their papers from Catherine's lentil problem and have each explain his or her method to someone else. I told them that I was giving them new partners for this activity so that they had someone to talk with who had used a different method.

"Your job," I told them, "is both to explain your method and try to understand your partner's method. If you got different answers, then try and work together to see which one is correct. If you absolutely can't figure it out together, then let me know."

I was pleased with the interactions I observed. Students were trying to explain their thinking to one another. I'm not sure what this particular experience accomplished for each child, but it was lively and had potential to help support their learning.

MENU ACTIVITY

Overview

Make a Shape

In this activity, children each draw a shape that they think can hold 35 Color Tiles. They test their shape by placing Color Tiles inside their shape, using 10 tiles of one color, then switching to another color, and so on. *Make a Shape* not only encourages children to count by 10s, it also provides experience with geometry and area measurement.

188

Make a Shape $\boxed{\text{I}}$

You need: Color Tiles

1. Draw a shape. You want to be able to cover the inside with 35 tiles.

2. Test by covering the inside of the shape with Color Tiles. Use 10 tiles of one color, then 10 of another, and so on, until it's covered.

3. Count the Color Tiles.

4. Record the number of tiles inside your shape.

5. Repeat the activity: Draw, Test, Count, Record.

From *Math By All Means: Place Value, Grade 2* ©1994 Math Solutions Publications

Before the lesson

Gather these materials:
■ Color Tiles
■ Blackline master of menu activity, page 188
■ Blackline master, *Make a Shape* Sample, page 189

Getting started

■ Show the class the blackline master *Make a Shape* Sample and explain that you think 35 tiles will cover the inside of the shape.

■ Model for the class how you'll test the shape. Place 10 tiles of one color inside your shape, then switch to another color and place 10 more, and continue this way until the shape is full. (It will *not* hold 35 tiles.)

■ Count the tiles by 10s. Have the children figure how many more or fewer would make exactly 35. Ask for suggestions about how to adjust the shape.

■ Take another sheet of paper and draw a shape that you think would be more likely to hold 35 tiles. Test it as you did with the other.

■ Review for the class the directions on the menu task.

FROM THE CLASSROOM

NOTE It's important to be correct when using language to describe mathematical ideas. In this case, a choice had to be made between "cover the shape" and "cover the inside of the shape." A square, as an example of the kind of shape this task calls for, is made up of four line segments that enclose a region. The region enclosed isn't the square; technically, it's the inside of the square. So it isn't correct to ask children to cover the shape. This may seem picky, and it is. But the language we use is important in that it influences the language children use.

I introduced the activity to the class by reading the directions aloud and modeling what to do. Because I was trying to encourage the students to look to the directions when they needed help, I focused their attention on a poster-size copy of the written task. I asked them to identify the kind of paper called for, the materials required, and whether the activity was for individuals or partners, and called on different children to respond.

"The directions give you all the information you need about what to do," I said, and then read the first direction: *Draw a shape that you think will take 35 tiles to cover the inside.* I began to draw a shape on a piece of unlined paper, commenting aloud as I did so. "It helps me to think about the different shapes I cut for the 0–99 puzzle," I said. "Those shapes give me ideas for the kind of shape I'd like to make."

I held up my shape to show it to the class and then read the next direction: *Test by covering the inside of the shape with Color Tiles. Use 10 tiles of one color, then 10 of another, and so on, until it's covered.*

I put my paper on the desk and began placing tiles inside my shape. Some of the children stood up at their seats so they could watch while I worked. I started with green tiles first, then switched to blue, and finally to red. I used ten green, ten blue, and four red tiles.

I continued reading the directions: *Count the Color Tiles.* Several children called out that there were 24.

"Raise your hand if you can explain how you know there are 24 tiles on my shape," I said.

I called on Molly. "Because 10 and 10 makes 20 and 4 more makes 24," she said.

"Does anyone have a different way of explaining?" I asked. There were no other responses.

I returned to the directions: *Record the number of tiles inside your shape.* I removed the Color Tiles and wrote the number 24.

"So what do you think I learned about the shape I made?" I asked the class.

"It's not big enough," Sarah said.

"You need one that uses more tiles," Jason added.

Linking assessment with instruction

"Here's a thinking question," I said. "How many more tiles do I need to use 35?" I wrote on the board as I asked the question:

> I used 24.
> I want to use 35.
> How many more do I need?

The idea of "How many more?" is difficult for children this age. I take every opportunity that comes up to have a class discussion about the idea to help children develop strategies for dealing with problems of this type. I called on Rudy first.

"I think it's 11," he said, "because if you add one more 10 to 24, you get 34, and then you need to add 1." I recorded on the board:

$$24 + 10 = 34$$
$$34 + 1 = 35$$

Next I called on Hassan. "I think it's 9," he said.

"Explain how you figured," I responded.

"Well," he said, "4 plus 5 is 9, so you need 9 more."

"I agree with you that 4 plus 5 is 9," I said, and wrote on the board:

$$4 + 5 = 9$$

"If I started with 24 tiles and add 9, how many tiles would I have?" I asked, and wrote on the board:

$$24 + 9 =$$

Hassan and several other children began to count on their fingers. Several responded, and there were a variety of answers, including 32, 33, 35, and 36.

"I'm not convinced," I said. "I hear different answers."

I called on Katy. She didn't respond to Hassan's idea, but had a different thought. This was fine with me, as it gave Hassan some time to think more about his solution.

"What I did," she said, "was count. I went 25, 26, 27, 28, 29, 30, 31, 32, 33, 34, 35. I ran out of fingers at 34 and had to go one more. So I know it's 11." I wrote on the board:

$$25, 26, 27, 28, 29, 30, 31, 32, 33, 34, 35$$

Then I counted the numerals to verify that there were 11. I then called on Seth.

"I kind of did it like Katy," he said, "but a little different."

"What did you do?" I asked.

"I know that if you have 24," he said, "you need 6 more to get to 30 because I counted 25, 26, 27, 28, 29, 30. Then you need 5 more to get to 35. And 6 and 5 makes 11." I recorded on the board:

$$25, 26, 27, 28, 29, 30$$
$$30 + 5 = 35$$
$$6 + 5 = 11$$

I called on Teddy next. "I think that 24 plus 9 is 33," he said, returning to Hassan's idea. "So you need 2 more to get to 35 and 9 plus 2 equals up to 11."

"What do you think, Hassan?" I asked.

"Yeah, that's right," he said, "you need 2 more." I wasn't sure that Hassan understood, but he seemed relieved and satisfied, so I didn't probe further.

"Any other ideas?" I said. Sarah raised her hand and came to the board.

"My mother taught me how to do this," she said, and wrote on the board:

$$24 + \underline{\quad} = 35$$

"Then you put the 11 on the line," she said.

"How do you know you're supposed to write 11 on the line?" I asked.

"I don't know, but I think it's right," she replied.

Molly claimed that both times she tried the activity she drew shapes that called for exactly 35 tiles.

Corrine's shape wasn't large enough for 35 tiles, but she did not attempt to figure out how many more she needed.

Several more hands were raised, but I told the children that I was going to stop the discussion. "I want to be sure that you understand the entire task," I said, "and then you can get to work. Remember that it doesn't matter if exactly 35 tiles cover the inside of your shape. It didn't for me. In this activity, you have the chance to draw a second shape and see if you can get closer to 35. And, if you'd like, you can try more shapes as well."

The children went to work on the menu. There were now six choices on the menu, and about eight of the children chose the new task. Some of the other children returned to an activity they'd done before, and others chose something new.

Observing the Children at Work

I noticed differences among the students as I observed them at work on this task. For example, some children placed tiles carefully inside the shape, nesting them close together with their edges touching. Other children, however, placed tiles with no regard to their position in relation to one another and were content even when some overlapped to the outside of the shape. Some students were bothered when some portion of the inside of the shape was left uncovered. Others were unconcerned and merely ignored the gaps.

Andrew indicated that his shape needed 5 more to hold 35 tiles.

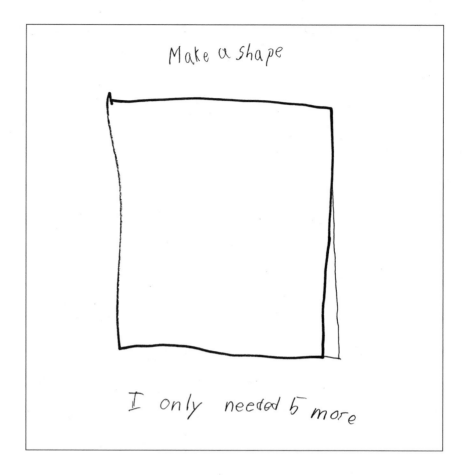

Make a shape

I only needed 5 more

As I circulated, I talked with children. I tried to help some see the importance of placing tiles together so that more of them would fit inside the shape. I talked with others about how they might deal with the spaces yet uncovered, tentatively encouraging them to think about halves of spaces, yet not pushing the idea if it didn't seem to make sense to the individual. I took note of different children's responses.

Some children were disturbed when exactly 35 didn't cover the inside of their shape. Some chose to adjust their shape so that 35 tiles covered the inside, either by redrawing lines and then rechecking, or by arranging 35 tiles and tracing around them. Other children seemed totally unconcerned when they didn't use 35 tiles and were happy to leave their papers as they were. I noted these differences as well.

Also, while some of the children followed the directions of the activity and used ten of one color and then switched to another color, others either arranged tiles in a color pattern that pleased them or merely chose tiles at random. I talked with students who weren't following the system of using ten of one color and then switching colors and pointed out its advantage. (After all, seeing the usefulness of grouping by 10s in a problem-solving situation was an underlying goal of this activity in the context of the unit.) I observed what the children did when I left them to get back to work by themselves and tried to judge their readiness and understanding.

MENU ACTIVITY

Five Tower Game

Overview

The *Five Tower Game* provides another way for children to generate a large number of objects to count. In this game, they use interlocking cubes. They take turns rolling the dice and making towers. After five turns each, they snap their towers into long trains, count the cubes in two ways, and compare who has more and who has less.

190

Five Tower Game

You need: Interlocking cubes
            2 dice

Rules:
1. Take turns. On your turn, roll the dice. The sum tells the number of cubes to take. Snap them into a tower.

2. Do this until you each have five towers.

3. Each makes a long train with your five towers. Count your cubes in two different ways.

4. Compare who has more and who has less. How many more does one have than the other?

5. Record.

Note: This activity, taught to a different class of children than described in this unit, appears on Part 2 of the videotape series *Mathematics: Teaching for Understanding*. (For information, see the Bibliography on page 193.)

Before the lesson

Gather these materials:
■ Blackline master of menu activity directions, page 190
■ Interlocking cubes, such as Multilink, Snap, or Unifix cubes
■ Two dice for each pair of children

Getting started

■ Show the class the cubes and the dice, and tell them they'll use the materials to build towers, then count their cubes two ways.

■ Model the game for the class by playing with a child or by having two children play with each other. Introduce the rules by reading them from the menu task.

■ Reinforce that they are to pay attention to what their partners are doing so they are sure they agree.

FROM THE CLASSROOM

To teach the *Five Tower Game,* I assembled a bucket of 3/4-inch interlocking cubes, two dice, and a poster-size copy of the directions. When I posted the directions, Timmy blurted out, "It's for partners!"

"Yes," I said, "the 'P' tells that it's for partners."

Andrew raised his hand. He had a suggestion. "You wouldn't have to put the 'P' in the corner if you listed 'partner' where it says 'You need,'" he said.

"The 'P' works," Nick countered. "It's good in the corner."

I thanked the boys for their suggestions and asked for their attention. "I'm going to teach the game by playing it with Annie," I said. "Please watch and listen so you can learn the rules." I read the beginning of the first direction: *To play: Take turns. On your turn, roll the dice. The sum tells the number of cubes to take. Snap them into a tower.*

I asked Annie to roll first and report the numbers to the class. "I rolled a 6 and a 5," she said.

"Raise your hand," I said to the class, "when you've figured out how many cubes Annie should take."

I called on Gwyn. "It's 11," she said.

"How do you know that?" I asked.

"I know it because I know that 5 plus 5 is 10 and you just need 1 more, so it's 11," she answered.

Usually, when children present their ideas for computing, I record their methods on the board to model for them how to use mathematical symbols to describe their thinking. But today I was more interested in getting on with my explanation of the game, so I merely accepted their verbal explanations.

"Did anyone figure it out a different way?" I asked. I called on Jason.

"I started with 5," he explained, "and I counted up like this: 6, 7, 8, 9, 10, 11." Jason demonstrated with his fingers.

"Is there another way?" I continued. I called on Amelia.

"I knew 6 plus 4 is 10," she said, "and then you plus 1 more and you get 11."

I'm always interested in hearing the variety of children's methods. We've had class discussions like this enough times previously so that the children knew that I would listen to all their different ideas.

NOTE It's important to convey to the class that there is no best or right way to calculate. Children should learn that what's most important is that their methods make sense to them and they can explain them so that others are also convinced they make sense. Adopt the practice of having children report their thinking in all situations. The payoff is that students learn that explaining their thinking is expected and they become more and more willing to do so.

I called on Andrew next. "I did it kind of like Gwyn," he began. "I took 1 from the 6 and made it 5 and then did 5 plus 5 and then added the 1 back on."

I called on Leslie next. "Mine is like Jason's, but different," she said. "I started with 6 and 5 more. I did 7, 8, 9, 10, 11."

Hassan reported next. "I just knew it," he said.

Nick had a new method. "I did 6 plus 6," he said, "and then you take away 1."

Grace reported last. Her method was a bit more involved. "I took 1 from the 5 and put it on the 6 and that made 7," she said. "Then I had 4 more, so I added 2 more, that made 8, 9, and then I added 2 more, and that made 10, 11."

No other children had suggestions, so I returned to teaching the game. During this time, Annie had snapped her 11 cubes together. I asked her to stand the tower up carefully and I took a turn. When I reported that I had rolled a 4 and a 2, I heard a chorus of "6." I built my tower.

"Let me read some more of the directions before Annie and I continue," I said, and read: *Do this until you each have five towers.*

Annie and I continued rolling dice and making towers. I didn't stop to discuss the sums of the two dice each time we rolled, as I wanted to move the game along. As Annie and I built our towers, some children commented on who they thought was winning. Finally, we each had built five towers.

I read the rest of the directions: *Each makes a long train with your five towers. Count your cubes in two different ways. Compare who has more and who has less. How many more does one have than the other?*

"That's like *Dollar Signs*," Katy said.

"How is it like *Dollar Signs*?" I asked.

"We had to count the dollar signs two different ways, too," she answered.

"I'll start by counting my cubes by 2s," I said. "Count along with me quietly." I pointed to the cubes as we counted. There were 36 cubes.

"I'm going to count them by 10s next," I said. "Raise your hand if you know how many 10s I'll have." More than half the class raised their hands. I called on Molly.

"You'll have three," she said.

"How do you know?" I asked.

"Because three 10s make 30," she answered.

"And you'll have six extras," Rudy called out.

"How do you know?" I asked.

"Because it's 36," he said, "and you need 6 more to make 30 into 36."

I carefully placed Annie's train next to mine.

"You win," Eli said.

"Annie doesn't have as many," Leslie said.

"How many more do I have?" I asked.

Several children who were close counted. "You have seven more," Eli said.

"How many cubes do you think there are in Annie's train?" I asked.

About two-thirds of the class seemed totally perplexed about how to figure this out. After a few moments, only six children had raised their hands. I called on Hassan.

"I think it's 31," he said.

"Explain how you figured," I said.

Leslie and Jason described the same game differently.

> five tower Game
>
> I counted by 5's and I got 38. and Jason got 38. I counted by 10's and I got 38.

> Five Twor game
> we got a ti I had 38
> She had 38.

Hassan shrugged. "I just guessed," he said.

"Listen to someone else's idea," I said, "and that may give you a way to think about how to solve the problem."

"It's 29," Andrew said. I can count on Andrew to give a correct answer and be able to explain his reasoning. "Because if you take away 6," he continued, "you have 30 and you have to take away 1 more and that makes 29."

"He's right," Annie said. She had counted the cubes.

"How many 10s can Annie make with her train?" I asked. Several children called out that there would be two 10s. Andrew disagreed.

"There would be almost three," he said. "Just one would be missing."

I ended my introduction at this point and asked the children to talk with their partners and decide which activity from the menu they would like to do. Six pairs of children chose the new activity. This level of interest is typical when I introduce a new activity.

The instructions for the activity didn't provide specific directions about the recording children were to do. As they worked, several children asked me about what they should write. I gave them my stock answer, "Use words, numbers, and, if you'd like, pictures." Children interpreted this in different ways.

Jason and Leslie were partners. After playing a game, Jason wrote: *We got a ti. I had 38. She had 38.* For the same game, Leslie wrote: *I counted by 5's and I got 38. and Jason got 38. I counted by 10's and I got 38.*

Sarah and Rudy were partners, and their papers revealed a collaboration that wasn't evident in Jason and Leslie's work. Sarah wrote: *I got 46 cubes and Rudy onley got 38. We played for about 2 minits it seemed liked. And ...... best of all I won!* Rudy wrote: *Sarah got 46 cubs and I got 38 cubs. I canted by 2's and 5's. I think it took abut 3 min. it seems like.* Both of them drew pictures of their towers of cubes.

Rudy included a drawing of the game he played with Sarah.

Some children included different kinds of information. For example, Amelia wrote: *Molly had 37 and I had 33. All together there was 70.* Hassan wrote: *I count by 2. I count by 5. Catherine got 41. She wun by 3.* He wrote *38* for his answer.

I like the differences among the children's work. They give me insights into children's responses to the activity and to their writing ability.

Hassan explained how he counted and how many more cubes Catherine had.

Five tower Game
I count by 2.
I count by 5.
catherine got 41.
she wun by 3.

38

Linking assessment with instruction

During menu time, as I circulate in the class and observe, I am available to assist children who have questions. Also, I intervene when I perceive children need encouragement to stay involved or are confused about directions. I also take opportunities to interrupt children when I see an opportunity to probe their thinking and informally assess their understanding.

Jonathan and Jason were partway through the *Five Tower Game* when I interrupted them. Each boy had made three towers.

"Who has more cubes right now?" I asked.

Each boy started to count his cubes. Jonathan counted 40 and Jason counted 27.

"He does," Jason said.

"Can you figure out how many more cubes Jonathan has?" I asked. This question was too difficult for them. Jonathan typically solves numerical problems either by counting concrete objects or by making tally marks on paper. He's not able to think about quantities merely from written numbers. Also, he doesn't use "counting on" as a strategy. Jason is at a similar level.

The boys connected each of their three towers into a long train, stretched them out side by side, and counted the extra cubes in Jonathan's train. Even though they worked carefully, they miscounted. I chose not to correct them, as the exact answer didn't seem important.

Once their cubes were connected into long trains, they had no way to continue with their game. Also, a piece of one of the trains had broken off and the boys began to argue about whose cubes they were. Jason grabbed them, Jonathan grabbed them back, and I could see we were headed for trouble. I think my questioning raised their level of stress.

"I'm sorry I messed up your game," I told the boys. "How about starting over so you both have a fresh start?" That suggestion seemed okay to them, and they began the game once again.

Deciding when to interrupt children and when to let them continue working on their own is a professional decision that isn't always easy to make. I'm not sure it was a good choice to interrupt the boys as I did. Although the interaction confirmed my understanding about their limited ability with numbers, it also made them uncomfortable. In a few minutes, however, they were back to work, fully engaged with the game.

On another day, after playing the *Five Tower Game,* Grace and Andrew dismantled their towers and returned the cubes to the bucket. Grace became upset because she realized that they hadn't counted the cubes in their trains and therefore didn't have the information to write about their results. Andrew, however, wasn't at all concerned. He'd just as soon avoid writing whenever possible. But Grace was persistent and called me over to help them solve the problem.

"Tell me about your game," I said.

"I won by 2," Andrew said. Grace nodded in agreement.

"Can either of you remember the numbers you rolled?" I asked.

"I can," Grace said. "First I rolled two 12s, then two 4s, and then a 5."

"Then I think you have enough information to solve the problem," I said. Now I had Andrew's interest. He loves problems like this one. Grace wasn't so confident. She likes working with numbers, and her mother gives her a good deal of practice at home, but she doesn't always transfer her skills to problem situations.

"Do I have to build my towers again?" she asked.

Andrew and Grace separately figured out how many cubes they each had in their trains.

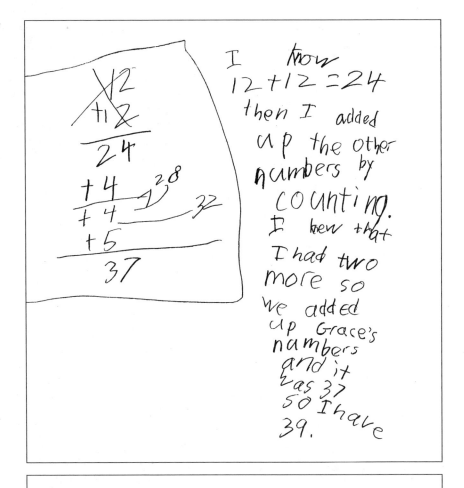

I know 12+12 =24 then I added up the other numbers by counting. I knew that I had two more so we added up Grace's numbers and it was 37 so I have 39.

$$12$$
$$+12$$
$$\overline{24}$$
$$+4$$
$$+4 \quad 28$$
$$+5 \quad 32$$
$$\overline{37}$$

I had double 12 and double 4. I had 15. all together is 37. My answer is 37. Andrew had 2 more then me so I think He has 39.

"You can if you want to," I answered.

"I don't think we need to," Andrew said, and he got up to get some paper.

"Can you help?" she asked.

"What sort of help would you like?" I asked.

"Maybe you could just sit here," she said.

I sat down at their table. Andrew returned with a piece of paper for each of them and they started to talk. Neither asked me for help. (I think perhaps the reassurance of my presence was helpful to Grace.)

While Grace and Andrew talked, I answered questions that other children brought to me. I then noticed that Grace and Andrew were working separately, each writing on a separate paper.

Finally, Grace interrupted me. "Is 33 right?" she asked.

"What's the question?" I asked.

Grace showed me her paper. She had written *12 plus 12, 4 plus 4, plus 5* on her paper. "I know that 12 and 12 is 24," she explained, "and then I counted and got 33."

"That's not right," I said. She recounted got 32, which I confirmed. She then added on 5, again by counting, and returned to work by herself.

Meanwhile, Andrew had completed his paper without any additional help from me. He figured out that Grace had 37 cubes in all and he, therefore, had 39. He wrote: *I know 12 + 12 = 24 then I added up the other numbers by counting. I knew that I had two more so we added up Grace's numbers and it was 37 so I have 39.*

Shortly afterward, Grace was finished. She had written: *I had double 12 and double 4. I had 15. all together is 37. My answer is 37. Andrew had 2 more than me so I think he has 39.*

MENU ACTIVITY

Guess My Number

Overview

Instead of using concrete materials, *Guess My Number* engages students in comparing the sizes of numbers. Most children this age are able to count to 100 (and beyond) and, given two numbers, tell which is greater and which is less. This game provides a way to reinforce children's familiarity with numbers.

Note: Although these skills are important, they aren't necessarily indicators of children's understanding of the place value structure of numbers. Children usually learn the pattern of the sequence of numbers before they understand the meaning of the positions of the digits.

191

Guess My Number

Rules:
1. Player 1 picks a number from 0 to 99 and writes it down.

2. Player 2 makes a guess and writes it down.

3. Player 1 gives a clue:

"Your guess is greater than my number."
or
"Your guess is less than my number."

4. Continue playing until Player 2 guesses the number.

5. Switch jobs and play again.

From *Math By All Means: Place Value, Grade 2*   ©1994 Math Solutions Publications

Before the lesson

Gather these materials:
■ Blackline master of menu activity, page 191
No other materials are needed for this activity. You may want, however, to have a 0–99 chart posted for children's reference.

Getting started

■ Tell the class you are going to teach them a guessing game.

■ Choose a child to be your partner to demonstrate the game, or play the game with the entire class acting as your partner.

■ Pick a number from 0 to 99 and write it on a piece of paper. Do not let the children see the number you chose.

■ Ask your partner (or someone in the class) to guess what your number might be. Respond to the guess with a clue: *Your guess is greater than my number* or *Your guess is less than my number.*

■ Continue until your partner has guessed your number.

■ You may want to play another game to be sure the children understand, or you may feel this isn't necessary.

■ Review the game by reading aloud the rules.

FROM THE CLASSROOM

The day before I planned to introduce this activity, Amelia and Molly asked me if they could try and figure out how to play *Guess My Number* from the directions on the task card. They had tried all the other activities on the menu and were interested in something new. I thought for a moment, couldn't think of a reason for them not to do so, and gave them permission.

By the end of math time, Amelia and Molly said they felt confident that they understood the activity. "It's a good one," Molly said. "The kids will like the guessing." Molly often positions herself in an adult-like way.

"Would you girls be interested in teaching the rules to the rest of the class?" I asked. They were excited by the idea.

"When?" Amelia asked.

"How about tomorrow?" I replied.

The girls grabbed each other, jumping up and down.

"You'll need to prepare," I said, to calm them. "You have to be sure you know the rules and have a way to help the others learn them."

"We can practice during lunch," Amelia said. They returned to their seats.

The Next Day

I began math class by telling the children that Amelia and Molly were going to introduce *Guess My Number*. The girls came to the front of the room, and Amelia began by coloring in the square in front of *Guess My Number* on the class list of menu activities.

The girls were shy. "We're going to show you how to play," Molly said in a soft voice. Molly looked at Amelia and neither of them seemed to know what do do.

NOTE One goal of math instruction is to help children learn to use correct mathematical language. It's common, however, for children to use words with which they are more comfortable. In *Guess My Number*, for example, children will often substitute "smaller," "littler," and "lower" for "less" or "bigger" and "higher" for "greater." Respond by continuing to use the preferred words. Teachers can best contribute to helping children become more familiar with correct language by modeling its usage.

"Who will guess first?" I said, to help them.

"I will," Amelia said.

"Okay," Molly said, coming to life a bit. "I pick a number and Amelia has to guess it."

"She gives me clues," Amelia added. "If my guess is too big, she says, 'Big,' and if it's too little, she says, 'Little.'"

"Can you say 'higher' and 'lower'?" Tomo asked.

"No," said Amelia, quickly and definitively.

I decided to intervene. "I think that Tomo's idea is okay," I said, "as long as his clues make sense to his partner. Tomo's words mean the same."

The girls continued. "Where should I write the number?" Molly asked me.

I suggested that she do so on the board under the corner of a poster that was tacked above. "That way," I said, "your number will be hidden from Amelia after you write it."

Amelia covered her eyes while Molly wrote the number "86." However, she reversed the "6" and some of the other students were confused.

"The '6' is backwards," I said to her softly. She fixed it.

"I'm going to write my guesses on the board," Amelia said. "That's the job of the guesser." Amelia's first guess was 89. As she wrote the "8" on the board, there was a gasp from the class. When she wrote the "9," they sighed with relief.

"Big," Molly said.

Next, Amelia guessed 57, not at all helped by the reaction from the class. She wrote 57 to the left of 89 and leaving a good deal of space in between them.

"Small," Molly said.

Amelia's next guess was 63, and she wrote it in between the 57 and the 89.

"Small," Molly said.

Amelia continued guessing and the class joined Molly in giving the clues. I stopped Amelia when she guessed 79.

"Before you guess again," I said, "can you tell me what you know for sure?"

Amelia looked at the information on the board. She had written all of her guesses in order of size. "It's 80."

"It doesn't have to be," Andrew called out. "It could be anywhere in the 80s."

"That's what I meant," Amelia said. She then guessed 81, skipped to 84, and worked her way up to 86. Molly showed her the answer.

"This game is like *Hot and Cold*," Abby said

During the presentation, Molly and Amelia were soft-spoken and a bit disorganized, and the rest of the class was a bit impatient. However, their introduction worked out fine in that the class understood how to play the game, and more than half chose it during menu time. The game was a popular one. Molly was right—the children enjoyed the guessing.

Linking assessment with instruction

As I interacted with children playing *Guess My Number*, I focused on their systems for keeping track of their guesses and on their strategies for guessing. In this way, I was assessing their logical reasoning skills more than their understanding of place value.

When Amelia and Molly had introduced the game, Amelia used a system for writing her guesses so that they were in numerical order. However, when I observed the children playing, I noticed that the children used a variety of record-keeping systems, some more useful than others.

Abby's system of recording was to write *B* or
L over each number to indicate whether the
guess was too big or too little.

Abby, for example, wrote the numbers in no particular order on her
paper. As Seth, her partner, gave her responses, she wrote "B" or "L"
above the numbers and put an "X" through them to show they were
wrong. When it was Seth's turn to guess, he attempted to write his guesses
in numerical order, listing them vertically. For his first game, he had difficulty spacing the numbers on the page and wound up with several lists of
numbers. After several games, however, he was able to place them more
efficiently. It was interesting to me to note that even after Abby and Seth
had played half a dozen games, neither paid attention to the other's system; each continued writing guesses in ways that made sense to them.

Seth tried listing his numbers in order, but his
system broke down as he made more guesses.

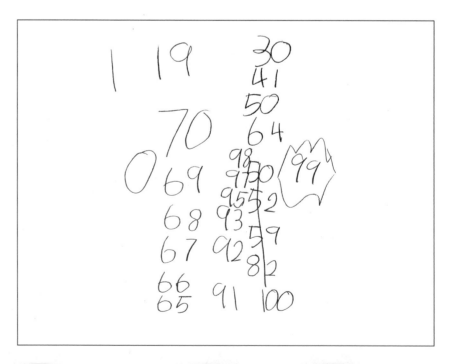

Colleen had a system, but it didn't help her with guessing. She numbered her guesses and listed them sequentially. Sometimes Colleen kept track of the clues she had received to zero in on the answer, but at other times she made seemingly random guesses that didn't give her any additional information. For example, after Colleen was given the clue that 45 was too big, she guessed 67. Her partner, Corrine, used her numbering system for guesses, but I didn't notice her making redundant guesses.

Corrine listed her guesses sequentially and numbered them.

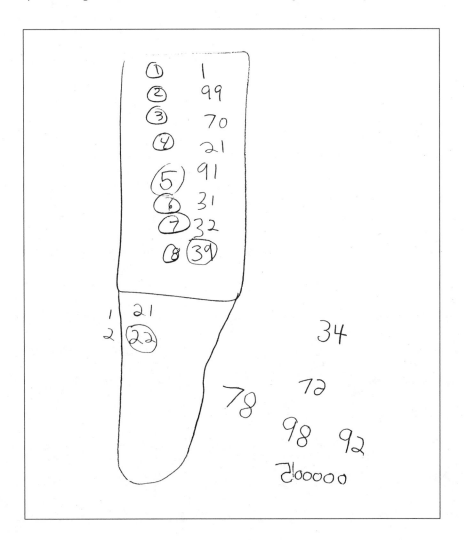

A Class Discussion About Record Keeping

One day, before the class went to work on the menu, I led a discussion about the game. I was interested in having children explain their record-keeping methods. I didn't want to imply that some methods were "better" than others, but I did want to encourage children to choose a system that helped them keep track of their thinking. Also, I wanted children to see alternatives to the systems they were using so they would learn that there are different ways to record. My goal was to reinforce for children that

they were to use methods that were useful and made sense to them.

"How are you keeping track of your guesses when you play?" I asked.

I called on Rudy. He explained his system, which was a variation of Seth's method of listing the numbers in order vertically. Rudy also explained how he chose numbers to guess. "I start with a number in the middle," he said, "and I write it in the middle of the paper. Then I have room to go up or down."

"What do you mean by a number in the middle?" I asked him.

"Like 40 or 50," he answered.

"So Rudy has a plan for making his first guess," I said. "A plan like that is called a strategy." I wrote the word "strategy" on the board. I planned to focus the children on strategies in a variety of ways throughout the year, and this was a good opportunity to introduce the word.

Maria raised her hand. "I like to start by guessing 99," she said.

"How come?" I asked. Maria just shrugged.

Sarah raised her hand. "I like to guess a big number, then a small number, like that," she said.

"Why do you do that?" I asked.

"I like it," she said. "It's like surrounding the number."

"What about other ways to record the numbers on your paper?" I asked.

Abby told how she wrote *B* or *L* above each guess. Then Teddy held up one of his papers to show how he crossed out numbers when they were wrong. "I don't cross them out a lot," he said, "because I still have to see them so I don't guess them again."

"I cross them out, too," Abby added.

Marina showed how she kept track of how many guesses her partner, Annie, made for each number. "It took her 22 guesses to guess 56," she said.

"What's the fewest number of guesses she needed?" I asked.

"I got 100 in only five," Annie said. Marina nodded her agreement.

I ended the discussion and asked the children to choose activities from the menu and begin their work. I wasn't sure that the class discussion met my pedagogical goals, but I'm often not sure of the effect of my conversations with second graders. I rely on later observations to provide evidence of the value of such a discussion.

CONTENTS

Draw Me a Star   168
The Go-Around Dollar   168
The King's Commissioners   169

CHILDREN'S BOOKS

Children's picture books have long been one of teachers' favorite tools for nurturing students' imaginations and helping them develop appreciation for language and art. In the same way, children's books that have a connection to mathematics can help students develop an appreciation for mathematical thinking. They can stimulate students to think and reason mathematically and help them experience the wonder possible in mathematical problem solving.

Each of the three children's books described in this section can add a special element to one or more of the activities in the Place Value unit. A synopsis and a reference to an activity in the unit are provided for each book.

Draw Me a Star
by Eric Carle
Philomel Books, 1992

Eric Carle was inspired to write this story by a drawing game he played as a child. He would draw an eight-pointed star over and over again, reciting a simple nonsense rhyme his German grandmother taught him: "Kri Kra Toad's Foot, Geese Walk Bare-Foot." *Draw Me a Star* begins with a young artist who draws a simple five-pointed star and then continues throughout his life to draw the sun, a tree, flowers, clouds, the moon, night, and, finally as an old man, the eight-pointed star as Eric Carle's grandmother taught him. The story captures children's imaginations, as do the bold and beautiful collages that illustrate the book.

After the young artist draws a five-pointed star, the star says to him, "Draw me the sun." The artist draws the sun, a large and warm sun with rays of bright yellow and orange.

"Draw me a tree, said the sun.

And the artist draws a tree.

It was a lovely tree.

Draw me a woman and a man."

The book continues: with requests for a house, a dog, a cat, and more.

At the end of the book, Carle presents a step-by-step procedure for drawing an eight-pointed star. Rather than include his grandmother's nonsense rhyme, he writes: "Down, over, left, and right, draw a star oh so bright."

An opportune time to read this book is during the *Stars in One Minute* whole class lesson. (See page 41.)

The Go-Around Dollar
by Barbara Johnston Adams
illustrated by Joyce Audy Zarins
Four Winds Press, 1992

In *The Go-Around Dollar*, Barbara Johnston Adams weaves a story about the travels of a single dollar with a collection of facts and anecdotes about the manufacture and use of dollar bills. In the story, Matt finds a dollar on his way home from school and uses it to buy shoelaces from Eric. Eric spends the dollar on bubble gum at the corner store and Jennifer receives the dollar as change. The story traces the dollar bill until it winds up posted as the first dollar earned in a new store. Information on each page tells children about the paper used to make dollars, the special inks used, the symbols on the front and back, the length of time a dollar stays in circulation, and more. Read this book to students after they've had some experience with *Race for $1.00.* (See page 92.)

The King's Commissioners
by Aileen Friedman
illustrated by Susan Guevara
A Marilyn Burns Brainy Day Book
Scholastic, 1994

In Aileen Friedman's book, the King has appointed a new royal commissioner every time a problem occurs in the kingdom. Among others, there is a Commissioner for Flat Tires, one for Chickenpox, and even one for Things That Go Bump In The Night. One day, the King decides that he needs to know how many royal commissioners he has altogether. He asks his two royal advisors to help him count the commissioners as they enter the throne room. The King begins to count one by one but loses count when the Princess comes home from school and interrupts him.

After all the commissioners enter the throne room, the First Royal Advisor explains that he counted by 2s, getting 23 groups of 2 and 1 more. The King is confused and complains, "That doesn't tell me anything!" The Second Royal Advisor counted by 5s, getting nine groups of 5 plus two more. The King responds in the same frustrated manner. Then the Princess steps in, has the royal commissioners line up in 10s, and counts four lines of 10 with seven left over: 47. Then she explains why the two royal advisors were also correct.

Read this book at the beginning of *The King's Commissioners* whole class lesson. (See page 72.)

CONTENTS

Stars in One Minute   172
Race for $1.00   172
Dollar Signs   173
Number Puzzle   174
Guess My Number   175

HOMEWORK

Homework assignments help children further their school learning and also give parents information about the kinds of activities their children are doing in school. The mathematics instruction that most parents experienced as children differs greatly from the instruction in this unit. Students' homework can serve as an effective way to communicate to parents about their children's learning.

Five ideas for homework are suggested. Each is presented in three parts:

Homework directions

This section explains the assignment and includes organizational suggestions when needed.

The next day

This section gives suggestions for using the assignment in the classroom. It's important that children know that work done at home contributes to their classroom learning.

To parents

A note to parents explains the purpose of the homework and the ways they can participate in their child's learning. These communications help parents understand more fully their children's math instruction.

HOMEWORK   Stars in One Minute

This homework should be assigned after the whole class lesson *Stars in One Minute*. (See page 41.)

Homework directions

Ask the children to time one minute while one of their parents, or someone else at home, draws stars. The children are to show their parents how they can count the stars in two different ways and bring the data to class the next day.

The next day

Distribute 3-by-3-inch Post-it™ Notes and have children record the data. Ask them to write their name, draw a sample of the star the person drew at home, and record the number of stars. Have them put the Post-its on the chalkboard.

As the children did with the data about their own stars, have them organize the Post-its into a graph to examine the different kinds of stars drawn at home. Discuss the differences between this graph and the class graph of the students' stars.

Or, you may want to add the Post-its with the information from home to the students' graph and discuss the changes in the shape of the data and the new conclusions that can be drawn.

To parents

> Dear Parent,
> Your child's homework assignment is to have you, or someone else at home, draw stars while your child times one minute. The purpose of the activity is to give children practice counting a large number of objects in several different ways. After you draw stars, ask your child to explain how to group and count them in at least two different ways.
>
> Your child has done this activity in class, and we've collected and organized the data from all the children. We will use the data the children bring from home to continue our statistical investigation.

HOMEWORK   Race for $1.00

This homework should be assigned after the menu activity *Race for $1.00*. (See page 92.)

Homework directions

Ask the children to teach someone at home how to play *Race for $1.00* and to play at least three games. Give them the information that they need 30 pennies, 20 dimes, and 2 dollars. You may want to duplicate play dollars and send them home.

Some students may not have dice at home. Show the children a substitute. Demonstrate cutting 12 slips of paper, numbering two each from 1 to 6, putting them in a bag, and drawing two out. Add the numbers on the two slips you drew to find out the number of pennies to take. Remind the students to replace the slips of paper in the bag each time before the next person's turn. Children may want to draw dots on the slips of paper to make them look more like dice.

The next day

Have children report about their experience playing the game at home, telling with whom they played and the responses they got.

To parents

> Dear Parent,
> *Race for $1.00* is a game that provides experience with exchanging pennies for dimes, thus relating the 10s and 1s structure of our number system to the real-life example of money. Please play at least three games with your child.
>   As you play the game, stop from time to time and ask your child to count up how much money you each have and compare the amounts to see who has more. Together, figure out how much more one person has than the other.

HOMEWORK

Dollar Signs

This homework should be assigned after the menu activity *Dollar Signs* (see page 101) and the homework assignment *Stars in One Minute.*

Homework directions

As the children did with stars, ask them to time one minute while one of their parents, or someone else at home, draws dollar signs. Have them bring the data to class.

The next day

Distribute 3-by-3-inch Post-it™ Notes and have children record the number of dollar signs drawn at home and put the Post-its on the chalkboard.
    Talk with the children about how to organize the Post-its into a graph. For this graph, don't focus on the differences among the dollar signs the parents drew, but instead on a way to organize the numerical counts. Discuss with the class the conclusions they can draw from the graph.

To parents

> Dear Parent,
> For one of the independent activities in our unit, students worked in pairs, taking turns timing one minute and drawing dollar signs. Please ask your child to time one minute while you draw dollar signs. Then have your child show you at least two different ways to group and count them.
>   Ask your child to bring your count to class for a statistical investigation.

HOMEWORK

Number Puzzle

This homework should be assigned after the menu activity *Number Puzzle.* (See page 129.)

Homework directions

Have the children take home their 0–99 puzzles to put together with their parents or someone else at home. Also, children in class can fill in another 10-by-10 grid with the numbers from 0 to 99 and glue the grid onto tagboard. They take it home and, with their parents, cut it into 10 to 12 pieces to make another puzzle for the class puzzle box. Remind students to write their name or initials on the back of each puzzle piece. Give each student a letter-size envelope to hold the new puzzle.

The next day

Have children report about their experience sharing their number puzzle and making a new one at home. You may want to give time for children to exchange puzzles and try to put them together.

To parents

> Dear Parent,
> Your child made the number puzzle by writing the numbers from 0 to 99 on a 10-by-10 grid and cutting it into pieces. Putting the puzzle together encourages children to look for patterns in the order of numbers. Work with your child to assemble the puzzle.
>   Your child also has an uncut 0–99 chart. Ask him or her to point out to you patterns in the numbers on the chart. Then, working together, cut the chart into 10 to 12 puzzle pieces, cutting only on the lines. Initial the back of each piece, put it in the envelope, and send it back with your child for our class puzzle box.

HOMEWORK

Guess My Number

This homework should be assigned after the menu activity *Guess My Number*. (See page 160.)

Homework directions

Have the children teach someone at home how to play *Guess My Number* and play at least three games.

The next day

Have children report about their experience playing the game at home, telling with whom they played and the responses they got.

To parents

Dear Parent,

Guess My Number focuses children on comparing the sizes of number from 0 to 99. One player chooses a number and the other player tries to guess it. The player who chose the number gives a clue, telling whether the guess was too large or too small. A game takes two rounds, with partners alternating between choosing a number and guessing the other person's number. Play at least three games with your child.

Along with providing experience with comparing numbers, the game also presents children with the opportunity to think logically. Talk with your child about his or her strategies for making guesses and keeping track of clues. Also, you might want to share your strategy with your child, but don't insist that your child use your method, even if it's more efficient than his or hers. There isn't one right or best strategy, and what's important is to encourage children to try different ideas when they play.

CONTENTS

Place Value Menu   178
0–99 Chart   179
0–99 Patterns (recording sheet)   180
Race for $1.00   181
Dollar Signs   182
Cover a Flat   183
0–99 Patterns   184
Number Puzzle   185
10-by-10 Grid   186
Fill the Cube   187
Make a Shape   188
Make a Shape Sample   189
Five Tower Game   190
Guess My Number   191
Play dollar bills   192

BLACKLINE MASTERS

The blackline masters fall into several categories:

Place Value Menu

This blackline master lists the titles of all the menu activities suggested in the unit. You may choose to enlarge and post this list for a class reference of the work to be done. Some teachers have children copy the list and make check marks or tallies each day to indicate the tasks they worked on; other teachers duplicate the blackline master for each child or pair of students.

Menu Activities

Nine menu activities are included. (They also appear in the text following the Overview section for each menu activity.) You may enlarge and post the menu tasks or make copies for children to use.

Worksheets

Blackline masters for three worksheets are included. Duplicate an ample supply of each and make them available to students.

Place Value Menu

☐ Race for $1.00

☐ Dollar Signs

☐ Cover a Flat

☐ 0–99 Patterns

☐ Number Puzzle

☐ Fill the Cube

☐ Make a Shape

☐ Five Tower Game

☐ Guess My Number

0–99 Chart

0	1	2	3	4	5	6	7	8	9
10	11	12	13	14	15	16	17	18	19
20	21	22	23	24	25	26	27	28	29
30	31	32	33	34	35	36	37	38	39
40	41	42	43	44	45	46	47	48	49
50	51	52	53	54	55	56	57	58	59
60	61	62	63	64	65	66	67	68	69
70	71	72	73	74	75	76	77	78	79
80	81	82	83	84	85	86	87	88	89
90	91	92	93	94	95	96	97	98	99

From *Math By All Means: Place Value, Grades 1–2*   ©1994 Math Solutions Publications

0–99 Patterns

0	1	2	3	4	5	6	7	8	9
10	11	12	13	14	15	16	17	18	19
20	21	22	23	24	25	26	27	28	29
30	31	32	33	34	35	36	37	38	39
40	41	42	43	44	45	46	47	48	49
50	51	52	53	54	55	56	57	58	59
60	61	62	63	64	65	66	67	68	69
70	71	72	73	74	75	76	77	78	79
80	81	82	83	84	85	86	87	88	89
90	91	92	93	94	95	96	97	98	99

Race for $1.00

You need: Zip-top baggie with 30 pennies, 20
         dimes, and 2 play dollars
         2 dice

Rules:
1. Take turns. On your turn, roll the dice. The sum
   tells how many pennies to take.

2. Decide if you want to exchange.
   (10 pennies = 1 dime)

3. Give the dice to your partner.

4. Play until one player has $1.00.

Notes:
1. You may exchange only when you have the dice.

2. Watch to make sure you agree with your
   partner's moves.

From *Math By All Means: Place Value, Grades 1–2*   ©1994 Math Solutions Publications

Dollar Signs

You need: A way to time one minute

1. One person times one minute, and the other person draws dollar signs ($).

2. Switch jobs.

3. After you've each drawn dollar signs, count how many you drew in two different ways.

4. Write about how you counted.

Cover a Flat

You need: 2 flats, 20 tens rods, 30 unit cubes, and a pair of dice

Rules:

1. Each takes one flat.

2. Take turns. On your turn, roll the dice. The sum tells how many unit cubes to take. Place them on your flat.

3. Decide if you want to exchange 10 unit cubes for a tens rod.

4. Give the dice to your partner.

5. Play until one player covers his or her flat.

Notes:

1. You may exchange only when you have the dice.

2. Watch to make sure you agree with your partner's moves.

From *Math By All Means: Place Value, Grades 1–2* ©1994 Math Solutions Publications

0–99 Patterns

$\boxed{\text{I}}$

You need: 0–99 patterns

1. Choose a 0–99 pattern, figure out the rule, and write it.

2. Check your answer. If you disagree, talk with the person who made the rule.

3. Do this for at least 5 patterns.

P.S. If you'd like, make other puzzles, put them in your folder, and I'll add them to the class supply.

From *Math By All Means: Place Value, Grades 1–2* ©1994 Math Solutions Publications

Number Puzzle

I

You need: a 0–99 number puzzle

1. Put the puzzle together to make a 0–99 chart.

2. Sign your name on the back of the envelope to show you solved it.

3. Put the pieces back into the envelope.

4. Do at least 5 people's puzzles.

From *Math By All Means: Place Value, Grades 1–2* ©1994 Math Solutions Publications

10-by-10 Grid

Fill the Cube

You need: 1 Unifix cube with tape on the bottom
1 baggie of popcorn
1 baggie of lentils

1. Estimate: How many kernels of popcorn do you think will fill the cube? Record.

2. Fill the cube with popcorn. Then count the popcorn at least two different ways. Record and explain how you counted.

3. Repeat: Now do it with lentils. Estimate, Count, Record.

4. Write: How did your two counts compare?

From *Math By All Means: Place Value, Grades 1–2* ©1994 Math Solutions Publications

Make a Shape

You need: Color Tiles

1. Draw a shape. You want to be able to cover the inside with 35 tiles.

2. Test by covering the inside of the shape with Color Tiles. Use 10 tiles of one color, then 10 of another, and so on, until it's covered.

3. Count the Color Tiles.

4. Record the number of tiles inside your shape.

5. Repeat the activity: Draw, Test, Count, Record.

From *Math By All Means: Place Value, Grades 1–2*   ©1994 Math Solutions Publications

Make a Shape Sample

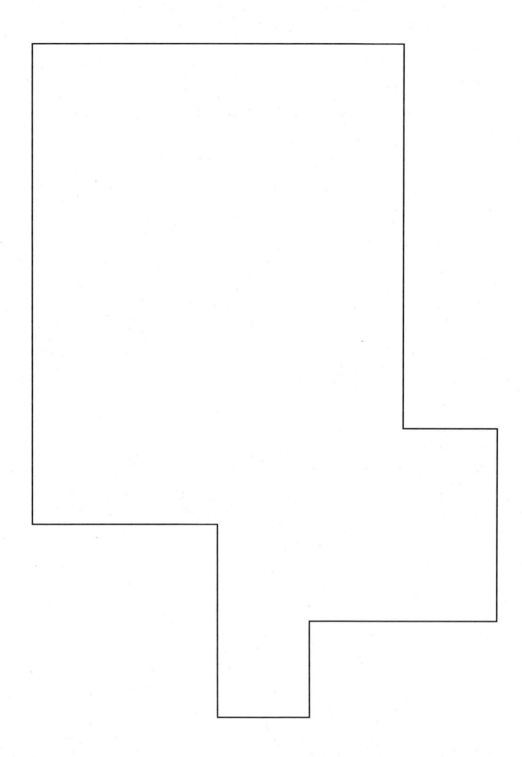

Five Tower Game

P

You need: Interlocking cubes
             2 dice

Rules:
1. Take turns. On your turn, roll the dice. The sum tells the number of cubes to take. Snap them into a tower.

2. Do this until you each have five towers.

3. Each makes a long train with your five towers. Count your cubes in two different ways.

4. Compare who has more and who has less. How many more does one have than the other?

5. Record.

From *Math By All Means: Place Value, Grades 1–2*   ©1994 Math Solutions Publications

Guess My Number

Rules:
1. Player 1 picks a number from 0 to 99 and writes it down.

2. Player 2 makes a guess and writes it down.

3. Player 1 gives a clue:

   "Your guess is greater than my number."
   or
   "Your guess is less than my number."

4. Continue playing until Player 2 guesses the number.

5. Switch jobs and play again.

From *Math By All Means: Place Value, Grade 2*   ©1994 Math Solutions Publications

BIBLIOGRAPHY

Adams, Barbara J. *The Go-Around Dollar.* Illustrated by Joyce A. Zarins. Four Winds Press, 1992.

*Burns, Marilyn. *Mathematics: Teaching for Understanding (K–6).* Set of three videotapes. Cuisenaire Company of America, 1992.

*—. *Mathematics: Assessing Understanding.* Set of three videotapes. Cuisenaire Company of America, 1993.

*Burns, Marilyn, and Bonnie Tank. *A Collection of Math Lessons from Grades 1 Through 3.* Math Solutions Publications, 1988.

Carle, Eric. *Draw Me a Star.* Philomel Books, 1992.

*Friedman, Aileen. *The King's Commissioners.* A Marilyn Burns Brainy Day Book. Scholastic, 1994.

Kamii, Constance. "Encouraging Thinking in Mathematics." *Phi Delta Kappan,* December 1982: 247–251.

National Council of Teachers of Mathematics. *Curriculum and Evaluation Standards for School Mathematics.* National Council of Teachers of Mathematics, 1989.

Russell, Susan Jo, and Rebecca B. Corwin. *Sorting: Groups and Graphs.* Used Numbers Series. Dale Seymour Publications, 1990.

Williams, Vera B. *A Chair for My Mother.* Greenwillow Books, 1982.

Other Books in the *Math By All Means* Series

*Burns, Marilyn. *Multiplication, Grade 3.* Math Solutions Publications, 1991.

*—. *Probability, Grades 3–4.* Math Solutions Publications, 1995.

*Confer, Chris. *Geometry, Grades 1–2.* Math Solutions Publications, 1994.

*Ohanian, Susan, and Marilyn Burns. *Division, Grades 3–4.* Math Solutions Publications, 1995.

*Rectanus, Cheryl. *Geometry, Grades 3–4.* Math Solutions Publications, 1994.

*These materials are available through: Cuisenaire Co. of America, Inc.
P.O. Box 5026
White Plains, NY 10602-5026
(800) 237-3142

INDEX

0–99 chart, 21, 22–40, 87, 88, 122–123, 129–130, 160

Activities. See Menu activities
Adams, Barbara Johnston, 93, 168, 193
Addition, 14, 18, 27–28, 36–40, 56–66
Algorithm, 36, 142
    Marina's, 38–40, 120, 144
Assessment
    10s and 1s relationship, 17, 67–71, 73
    addition, 18, 27, 36–40, 116–121, 140–145
    as an ongoing process, 13
    classroom experience with, 19–20, 27, 36–40, 67–71, 78, 116–121, 140–145
    Catherine's Problem, 138–139, 140–145
    description of, 3–4
    How Many 10s?, 67–71
    How Much Is Covered?, 116–121
    individual, 15, 16, 17–20
    informal, 27, 73, 78, 106
    instructions for, 36, 67, 116, 140
    introduction to, 13–16

    linking with instruction, 15–16, 95–100, 105–109, 113–115, 125–128, 132–133, 137–139, 148–151, 157–159, 162–165
    Numbers on the 0–99 Chart, 36–40
    on-demand, 16
    writing in, 13, 16, 68–71, 116–121, 140–144

Base Ten Blocks, 110–115
Bibliography, 193
Blackline masters, 177–192
Books, children's, 4, 167–169

Carle, Eric, 42, 46, 168, 193
Calculator use, 7, 27, 54–55, 117–118
Children's books, 4, 167–169
Chair for My Mother, A, 57, 193
Color Tiles, 146–151
Collection of Math Lessons, A, 57, 193
Cooperative learning, 4–5, 29, 85
Counting, 13–14, 18–20, 41, 56–57, 63–64, 72, 134–135, 140, 146, 152
Cubes, interlocking, 56–71, 107–108, 152–159

Daily schedule, suggested, 7–11
Draw Me a Star, 42, 46, 168, 193

Estimating, 134–135, 146–147

Friedman, Aileen, 72, 169, 193

Go-Around Dollar, The, 93, 168, 193
Geometry, *v*, 146
Graphing, 41, 43, 49–55
Grouping by 10s, 65–66, 67–71, 72–73, 75, 78–80, 104–105, 142–143, 146–147
Guess My Rule, 23, 28–35

Homework, 172–175
Hundreds number wall chart, 7

Individual interviews, 15, 16, 17–20

Kamii, Constance, 18, 193
King's Commissioners, The, 72–82, 169, 193

Letter to parents, 11, 172, 173, 174, 175
Letters to visitors, 91
Linking Assessment with Instruction, 15–16, 95–100, 113–115, 125–128, 157–159

Manipulative material
    Base Ten Blocks, 110–115
    Color Tiles, 146–151
    cubes, interlocking, 56–71, 107–108, 152–159
    Multilink cubes, 56, 152–159
    Snap cubes, 56–71, 107–108, 152–159
    Unifix cubes, 56, 134–135, 152–159
Materials and supplies, 6–7
Mathematical language, using correct, 147, 162
Mathematics: Assessing Understanding, 16, 18, 193
Mathematics: Teaching for Understanding, 22, 41, 92, 101, 152, 193
Measurement, v, 134, 146
Menu activities
    0–99 Patterns, 87–88, 122–128
    benefit of, 136
    classroom experience with, 84–91, 93–100, 102–109, 111–115, 123–128, 130–133, 135–139, 147–151, 153–159, 161–166
    Cover a Flat, 110–115, 116
    description of, 3, 83–84
    Dollar Signs, 101–109, 173
    Fill the Cube, 134–139, 140
    Five Tower Game, 152–159
    Guess My Number, 160–166, 175
    instructions for, 92–93, 101–102, 110–111, 122–123, 129–130, 134–135, 146–147, 152–153, 160
    introduction, 83–91
    Make a Shape, 146–151
    materials needed, 93, 102, 111, 123, 130, 135, 147, 153, 160
    Number Puzzle, 129–133, 174
    organizing, 5
    Race for $1.00, 86–87, 92–100, 110, 172

Money
    activities using, 83–89, 92–109
Multilink cubes, 56, 152–159

NCTM *Curriculum and Evaluation Standards for School Mathematics,* 1

Parents
    providing information for, 11
    sample letters to, 11, 172, 173, 174, 175
Patterns, 22–35, 122–123, 160
Place value
    10s and 1s structure, 1, 14, 17, 22, 56, 60, 67
    grouping by 10s, 65–66, 67–71, 72–73, 75, 78–80, 104–105, 142–143, 146–147
    NCTM Standards, 1
    number system, 1–2, 14, 17–18, 22, 83, 92
    regrouping, 14, 27, 36, 110, 141
    spatial model, 110
    understanding of, 14

Schedule, suggested daily, 7–11
Silent star, 26–27
Snap cubes, 56–71, 107–108, 152–159
Statistical data. See Graphing
Suggested daily schedule, 7–11

Time, measuring, 41–43, 101

Unifix cubes, 56, 134–135, 152–159
Used Numbers, 28,

Videotapes
    Mathematics: Assessing Understanding, 16, 18, 193
    Mathematics: Teaching for Understanding, 22, 41, 92, 101, 152, 193
Visitors, 91

Whole class lessons
    0–99 Chart, 22–35, 36, 122, 129
    classroom experience with, 24–35, 43–55, 57–66, 73–82
    Counting Fish, 56–66, 67, 72
    description of, 2–3, 21
    King's Commissioners, 72–82
    Stars in One Minute, 41–55, 56, 101, 172
    teaching instructions for, 22–23, 41–43, 56–57, 72–73
William, Vera B., 57, 193
Writing
    in assessment, 13, 16, 68–71, 116–121, 140–144
    errors by students, 6, 69, 126
    in math class, 6
    system for recording, 5–6
    usefulness of, 79